G. E Jaques

Chronicles of the St. James St. Methodist Church, Montreal

From the First Rise of Methodism in Montreal to the Laying of the....

G. E Jaques

Chronicles of the St. James St. Methodist Church, Montreal
From the First Rise of Methodism in Montreal to the Laying of the....

ISBN/EAN: 9783337162511

Printed in Europe, USA, Canada, Australia, Japan

Cover: Foto ©ninafisch / pixelio.de

More available books at **www.hansebooks.com**

CHRONICLES

OF THE

St. James St. Methodist Church

MONTREAL,

From the First Rise of Methodism in Montreal to the Laying of the Corner-Stone of the New Church on St. Catherine Street.

BY

G. E. JAQUES, Jun

TORONTO:
WILLIAM BRIGGS, 78 & 80 KING STREET EAST.
1888.

AUTHOR'S PREFACE.

ON leaving old St. James Street Church, many of the members thought that there were facts in its history worthy of being placed on record. It has in its time done much to aid other churches and church enterprises, and has had among its members many who have worked nobly in their Master's cause.

At the request of the Trustees, I have undertaken to chronicle some of the more important events of its history, and this little volume is the outcome of my labors. No attempt has been made at any literary ability, but rather to place before the present members some short, concise statements of what has been done in the past.

The historical part has been largely compiled by the late Rev. John Borland, from notes of the late John Mathewson, Dr. Carroll's "Case, and His Cotemporaries," as well as from his own knowledge, he having been pastor of the church in the years 1841 and 1842.

G. E. JAQUES, Jun.

Our Pastors.

1803.

S. MERWIN.
M. RUTER.
S. COATES.
NATHAN BANGS.
T. MADDIN.
J. SCULL.
J. MITCHELL.
T. BURCH.
R. WILLIAMS.
J. B. STRONG.
J. DePUTRON.
W. BROWN.
J. BOOTH.
W. BARLOW.
R. POPE.
R. L. LUSHER.
E. BOWEN.
A. SIEGER.
J. HICK.
T. DIXON.
J. KNOWLAN.
H. POPE.
R. ALDER, D.D.
J. STINSON.
WILLIAM SQUIRE.
W. CROSCOMBE.
JOHN BARRY.
W. LORD.
W. M. HARVARD.
J. B. SELLEY, M.D.
E. BOTTERELL.
R. HUTCHINSON.
J. B. BROWNELL.
J. P. HETHERINGTON.
M. LANG.
J. BORLAND.
R. COONEY.
C. CHURCHILL, M.A.
GEO. H. DAVIS.
MATTHEW RICHEY, D.D.
C. CHURCHILL, M.A.

1846.

Our Pastors.

1847.

MATTHEW RICHEY, D.D.
C. CHURCHILL, M.A.
JOHN JENKINS, D.D., LL.D.
C. DeWOLFE.
LACHLIN TAYLOR, D.D.
WM. SQUIRE.
G. N. A. F. T. DICKSON.
GEO. DOUGLAS, D.D., LL.D.
J. H. BISHOP.
WELLINGTON JEFFERS, D.D.
JOHN GEMLEY.
ISAAC B. HOWARD.
EPHRAIM B. HARPER, D D.
JAMES ELLIOTT, D.D.
CHARLES LAVELL, M.A.
WILLIAM BRIGGS, D.D.
J. B. CLARKSON, M.A.
ALEX. SUTHERLAND, D.D.
BENJAMIN LONGLEY, B.A.
LEONARD GAETZ.
HUGH JOHNSTON, M.A., B.D.
E. D. MALLORY.
JOHN POTTS, D.D.
JOHN PHILP, M.A.
JAMES HENDERSON.

1888.

ST. JAMES STREET METHODIST CHURCH

Pastor, REV. JAMES HENDERSON.

Residence, - - 18 UNIVERSITY STREET.

SERVICES.

SUNDAY, 11 a.m.; 7 p.m.

SUNDAY SCHOOLS. Morning, meets 9.30 a.m. Superintendent: WM. HODGSON.

Afternoon school meets at 3 p.m. Superintendent: HON. JAMES FERRIER. Assistants: JAMES FERRIER, jun., and W. C. PALMER.

BIBLE CLASSES for ladies and gentlemen. Conducted by REV. J. H. STEVENSON.

YOUNG MEN'S CLASS. Conducted by A. O. DAWSON.

YOUNG LADIES' BIBLE CLASS. Conducted by GEORGE FORBES.

INFANT CLASS. Conducted by Miss NICHOL and Miss ARCHIBALD.

WEEK-NIGHT MEETINGS.

Monday, Young People's Association. Rev. J. Henderson, President; C. S. Babcock and Miss Ball, Vice-Presidents; J. A. Vibert, Secretary; J. Ferrier Torrance, Treasurer.

Wednesday, Preaching Service.

Friday, Christian Workers' Association. David Watson, President.

Saturday, Young Men's Meeting. A. O. Dawson.

SOCIETY CLASSES.

Sunday, 10 a.m.
- James McBride.
- James A. Mathewson.
- D. Cameron.
- J. Ferrier, jun.

Sunday, 3 p.m.
- George Armstrong.
- D. T. Frost.
- E. Wethey.

Monday, 3 p.m. The Pastor's Class.

Tuesday, 3 p.m.
- Hon. James Ferrier.
- Mrs. Seybold.

Thursday, 3 p.m.
- Miss Campbell.
- Mrs. W. E. Ross.
- Miss Douglas.

Thursday, 8 p.m. { John Torrance. Alf. Evans. J. G. Parks. Edward T. Wilkes. George Forbes.

Friday, 8 p.m. { John Donaghy. David Lund.

MEMBERS OF QUARTERLY OFFICIAL BOARD.

Ministers: Rev. James Henderson; Rev. George H. Davis, (Peterboro', Ont.); Rev. George Douglas, LL.D.

Local Preachers and Exhorters: J. B. Waid, M.D.; James A. Mathewson; Thomas Nichol, M.D., D.C.L., LL.D.; J. Thompson; Arthur O. Dawson; Wm. C. Palmer; J. T. Smith.

Stewards: John Torrance; Geo. E. Jaques, jun.; John Murphy; Jos. E. Alston; Robert Miller; Wm. Armstrong; John Cowan.

Class Leaders: Hon. Senator Ferrier; James A. Mathewson; John Torrance; J. Ferrier, jun.; Alderman James McBride; George Armstrong; George Forbes; D. T. Frost; D. Cameron; D. Lund; E. Wethey; Alfred Evans; J. G. Parks; Edward T. Wilkes; Jno. Donaghy; Mrs. Ross; Miss Campbell; Miss M. Douglas; Mrs. Doran; Mrs. Seybold.

Representatives: David Watson; Alderman James Griffin; T. W. Burdon; W. L. Lee; George Lamb; John Rogers.

Superintendents of Sunday Schools: Hon. James Ferrier; Wm. Hodgson; W. Godbee Brown.

TRUSTEES OF ST. JAMES STREET CHURCH.

Appointed March 23rd, 1844.

John Torrance.
David Torrance.
James Ferrier.
William Lunn.

John Mathewson.
John Hilton.
Richard Latham.
Thomas Kay.

Robert Campbell.

TRUSTEES OF ST. CATHERINE STREET CHURCH.

Appointed March, 1886.

Hon. James Ferrier.
Thos. D. Hood.
George Armstrong.
John Torrance.
George Young.
Frederick Fairman.
Rev. George Douglas, LL.D.
James McBride.

George Vipond.
George E. Jaques, jun.
Dugald Graham, B.C.L.
Thomas Nichol, M.D., D.C.L.,
James Griffin.   [LL.D.
Robert Miller.
J. E. Alston.
James Ferrier, jun.

Alfred Ward.

ST. JAMES STREET METHODIST CHURCH.

Officers and Teachers of the Sunday Schools in Connection with St. James Street Methodist Church.

REV. JAMES HENDERSON, Pastor.

ST. JAMES STREET AFTERNOON SCHOOL—3 P.M.

Officers.

Hon. Jas. Ferrier, Superintendent.
Jas. Ferrier, jun., 1st Ass't "
W. C. Palmer, 2nd   "   "
Thomas W. Burdon, Secretary.
Frank B. Siegars Ass't   "
A. D. Evans, Missionary Secretary.
Thomas Nichol, jun., Ass't   "

David Watson, jun., } Associate
J. H. L. Dunn,   } Organists.
Ed. T. Wilkes, Librarian.
J. Ferrier Torrance, } Associate
W. H. Davidson,   } Librarians.
J. A. Mathewson, jr. }
A. O. Dawson, Treasurer.

Teachers.

George Hoggard.
George Forbes.
George Kimber.
Hugh King.
John Vibert.
Duncan Cameron.
R. McFarlane.
J. B. McConnell, M.D.
A. O. Dawson.
F. Shaver.
Wm. McLaughlin.
Robert W. Evans.
J. H. L Dunn.
J. H. Stevenson.
Joseph Vibert.
J. Todd.
Geo M. P. Bogan.
Wm. Philp.

Mrs. Cowan.
 "   Graham.
 "   Atkinson.
Miss Ferrier.
 "   Hodgson.
 "   Florence Hodgson.
 "   Patton.
 "   C. Dawson.
 "   A. S Dawson.
 "   Cockburn.
 "   Carlisle.
 "   Borland.
 "   Macfarlane.
 "   Nichol.
 "   Mathewson.
 "   M. E. Jaques.
 "   Archibald.
 "   A. L. Dawson.
 "   M. E. Allen.
 "   Ida Graham

ST. JAMES STREET MORNING SCHOOL—9.30 A.M.

Officers.

Wm. Hodgson, Superintendent.
John Murphy, Ass't   "
W. G. Brown, Treasurer.
E. H. Liversedge, Secretary.
Geo. Smith, Ass't Secretary.

C. S. Babcock, Missionary Secy.
Geo. Moffatt, Ass't   "   "
C. Frost, Librarian.
Robt. Brown, Ass't Librarian.
Miss Murphy, Organist.
J. T. Edward, Ass't Organist.

Teachers.

Geo. Hoggard.
John Bonner.
W. G. Brown.
Geo. Lamb.
John Murphy.
W. Morris.
Mr. Finch.
J. Todd.
W. McLaughlin.
J. W. Runions.

Miss Lund.

P. Richardson
Miss Frost.
 " Warcup.
 " Ball.
 " Longmoor.
 " Bastian.
 " Fox.
 " Innes.
 " Hodgson.
 " Hudson.

DESRIVIERES STREET MISSION SCHOOL—3 P.M.

Officers.

W. G. Brown, Superintendent.
J. W. Duffie, Ass't " and Treas.

W. H. Punchard, Secretary.
Miss Craig, Organist.

Teachers.

J. W. Duffie.
W. S. Lingley.
Jas. Smith.

Miss McVey.

R. H. Clerk, B.A.
W. L. Lee.
Miss Dier.

NUMBER ON ROLL BOOKS.

	Male.	Female.	Total.
Officers and Teachers—Afternoon School	31	20	51
Morning "	19	11	30
Desrivieres "	7	3	10
Total for three schools	57	34	91
Scholars—Afternoon School	188	227	415
Morning "	120	151	271
Desrivieres "	36	45	81
Total for three schools	344	423	767

AMOUNT RAISED FOR MISSION PURPOSES DURING THE YEAR.

Afternoon School $674 57
Morning School 334 54
Desrivieres School 103 75

$1,112 86

ST. JAMES STREET METHODIST CHURCH.

SCRIPTURE VERSES COMMITTED TO MEMORY DURING THE YEAR.

Afternoon School	23,358
Morning School	33,796
Desrivieres School	2,563
	59,717

NUMBER OF VOLUMES IN LIBRARY.

Afternoon School	600
Morning School	300
Desrivieres School	325
	1,225

The teachers and officers of the three schools, together with Messrs. Jas. A. Mathewson; E. Wethey; John Cowan; D. T. Frost and G. E. Jaques, jun., appointed by the Quarterly Board, form the Sunday School Committee of the Circuit.

LADIES' AID SOCIETY.

President	Mrs. Torrance.
Vice-President	Mrs. Fairman.
Secretary	Miss F. Hodgson.
Treasurer	Mrs. Nichol.

BAZAAR COMMITTEE.

President	Mrs. G. E. Jaques.
Secretary	Mrs. Jas. McBride.
Treasurer	Mrs. Jas. Griffin.

DORCAS SOCIETY.

President	Mrs. John Cowan.
Secretary	Miss Libby Longmore.
Treasurer	Miss Ellen Mathewson.

CHRONICLES

OF THE

St. James Street Methodist Church,

MONTREAL.

THE rise and progress of any interest that has become great, and that in its growth has exerted a deep and abiding influence for good upon large and varying communities of people, cannot fail to be interesting to every thoughtful and reflecting mind. Such is found to be true in reference to Methodism, the name given to the revival of religion which in the last century originated, and for many years was carried on, mainly through the labors of the Wesleys and Whitefield. Several valuable histories of this revival have been given to the world; and no desire need be felt, for the present at least, to add to their number. And yet this, by no means, renders it unnecessary, or out of place, to record the annals of a particular Church, such as would have but a very limited reference, if, indeed, they would have any at all, in a general history, however good and fair its narrations might be. For as a city may have facts which its citizens might desire to have faithfully recorded, without any expectation that such would have a place in a history of its nation, so a Church may, to its people, have a number of deeply interesting facts, worthy, in their judgment, of a fairly marked record, but which none imagine that in anything like the particularity and fulness they desire, would appear in a more general history of their denomination.

And this is precisely the case with the St. James Street Methodist Church of Montreal, which from the earliest years of the century has filled a high and important place, not only in the judgment and esteem of the Methodist people throughout Canada, but also in the United States, in Europe, and indeed almost everywhere that the parent or sister Churches of the Methodist people have extended and are applying their evangelistic operations.

The first visit to Montreal of any Methodistic agency was made by the Rev. Joseph Sawyer, of the New York Conference, in 1803. He was then laboring in the Bay of Quinte Circuit, in Upper Canada. He came to see "if a minister could be prudently stationed in this city." He found, we are told, a small society of seven members. It is said, this little society had been for some seventeen years in existence, but that, owing to the absence of ministerial oversight, it had not grown. How it originated we have no means of determining; the probability is that it was an offshoot from Quebec, where a military man of the name of Tuffy had labored as a local preacher. During the period of his regiment's stay in Quebec, which was for several years, and not long after the capitulation, when Canada first became a British possession, Mr. Tuffy, who appears to have been a commissariat officer, labored, with a measure of success, evidently; and in all probability he was the first Methodist preacher that lifted up the Gospel standard in Canada, and that Quebec was the first place in which the Gospel through its ministry won souls to Christ.

The following year, 1804, the Rev. Samuel Merwin, of the New York Conference, came to Montreal to make it his field of labor; but it does not appear that anything in the way of forming a society, or Church, was attempted until the following year, when the Rev. Martin Ruter was the minister in charge, and his membership is said to have been twelve.

ST. JAMES STREET METHODIST CHURCH.

Mr. Ruter continued to labor in Montreal through a second year, when the membership rose to twenty. At this number it seems to have stood for the three following years, and its ministers were the Rev. Samuel Coates, and the Rev. Nathan Bangs. Mr. Coates says, " that the building of a church in Montreal was first suggested ;" but that, beyond a suggestion, nothing was then done ; for we find that in the following year, 1806, Mr. Bangs, then stationed in Montreal, hired a room in which to hold divine service. He had been previously stationed in Quebec, and exchanged with Mr. Coates. In his life, referring to this appointment, he says : " At this time I sent for my wife, and we both pursued with some success, but with many difficulties, our pastoral labors. The society was poor, and numbered but twenty, and I had to grapple with many embarrassments ; but through all God supported me, and now, half a century later, I still praise Him for His goodness to me then." Mr. Bangs further remarks that, upon a calculation of his receipts and expenditures for the year 1806, he found that his expenses had exceeded his income by forty dollars.

In 1807, Mr. Bangs was appointed to the Niagara Circuit, in Upper Canada, and on his way there was met by his presiding elder, at whose instance he returned to Montreal, where he resumed his labors for another year. His residence in Canada altogether was about seven years ; in which time he says, "he had visited every city, town and village, and almost every settlement"—meaning, it may be supposed, those of Upper Canada, with the cities of Quebec and Montreal, in Lower Canada—"that he had travelled in Upper Canada through its forests and scattered settlements, and I believe that I am the first Methodist preacher that ever attempted to preach in L'ttle York (now Toronto). I preached in a miserable, half-finished house, on a week evening, to a few people—for there were not over half a dozen houses in the place—and slept on the floor under a blanket." This was in 1801. Canadian Methodism must ever recognize Mr. (subsequently Dr.) Bangs among its chief founders.

Of Dr. Bangs Dr. Stevens says, that "he did more to advance the interests of his denomination than any man of his day." From Dr. Carroll's work, "Case, and His Cotemporaries," we gather the following facts of this distinguished man : He was born in the Eastern States in 1779, where he received a good New England common-school education, and from his father he learned the art of surveying. In May, 1799, he started, accompanied by a devoted sister and her husband, for the wilds of Canada, in their journey to which they passed through what has since become the city of Buffalo, but was then not worthy the designation of a village, as there were not more than two or three log huts in the place. They crossed into Canada at Fort Erie, and settled in the vicinity of the great Cataract. Here, through the instrumentality of the Rev. Joseph Sawyer, he was converted, and led to join the Church. In the year 1801-2 he entered the ministry, and became assistant to his father in the Gospel, Mr. Sawyer. Many discouragements marked his early ministry, but soon an extensive revival, when over three hundred souls were converted, rewarded his faithful and persevering earnestness. Through the vast range of country known as Upper Canada, and for the period of seven years, as previously stated, Mr. Bangs continued his labors with varying success, but always with such attestations of divine influence as showed that he labored not in vain, and that the Gospel he preached was the power of God unto salvation to all that believed. One of the trustees of our new church saw Dr. Bangs, at a great camp-meeting in the United States, in 1853. He describes him as tall of stature, massive in his build, impressive in his appearance, with a warm and genial manner, and evident signs of great courage and strength of character, which doubtless served him well in his pioneer labors in this country.

Two other names occur connected with the early history of Methodism in Montreal, viz., those of Samuel Merwin and Martin Ruter, who subsequently became distinguished ministers in the Church of their brethren in the United States, and of whom, from Dr. Carroll's work, the following facts are supplied:

"Samuel Merwin was born in Durham, Con., September, 1777, and when but a mere lad was converted to God. Immediately after his conversion he began to declare what God had done for his soul, and to exhort his neighbors to flee from the wrath to come. When but twenty years of age, he entered the itinerant work, in which he continued until the year 1839, when he departed in peace to his reward in the skies. His personal appearance in the pulpit was unusually commanding; his voice melodious, clear and strong; and he spoke not only with eloquence, but in demonstration of the spirit and of power; and many souls were the seals of his ministry."

The other name, that of Martin (afterwards Dr.) Ruter, is that of the minister who in 1804 succeeded Mr. Merwin in Montreal, and who appears as the first who reported a membership there. "He was born in Charlestown, Mass. He became a subject of renewing grace in 1799, and joined the Church. In 1800 he obtained a license to preach, and in the following year he was admitted on trial by the New York Conference. In 1804 he was sent to Montreal, being then only nineteen years of age. He stood for Montreal for the years 1804-5, and then returned to labour in the States. He occupied important stations and positions in different parts of the great country of his birth and parentage, and closed his useful and honorable career by a peaceful death, cheered by a firm hope of heaven, in the fifty-third year of his age, and the thirty-seventh of his ministry."

His biographer says: "Dr. Ruter was no ordinary man. His early advantages were no more than a common-school education, and the period that other young men usually take for college degrees he spent in passing through the grades of an itinerant minister. Yet, in the itinerant ministry, Dr. Ruter became a literary man, well-versed in languages, science, and history, and discharged the duties of College President with great dignity."

In 1805, it was proposed to build a church in Montreal, yet nothing was done towards it until 1807, when Mr. Coates visited England, and obtained the greater part of the funds necessary for that object.

The building was then commenced, and also a dwelling-house for the minister, who, according to "Cornish's Hand-book," was the Rev. Thomas Maddin. The membership was thirty. This church was built in what is known as St. Sulpice Street, and where it yet stands, though much altered in appearance since it passed into the hands of the Roman Catholics. One of the most prominent of the trustees was the late Mr. John Torrance, who subscribed largely not only to this church, but also to the subsequent one, on the site of which is now erected the Medical Hall.

It is to be regretted that we have but little on record of the Church in Montreal in these early days. The Rev. Thomas Madden was followed by the Rev. Joseph Scull, who appears to have been the minister in charge for the years 1809 and 1810, and by Rev. J. Mitchell in 1811. The membership reported as being in each of these years, 1809 and 1810, at twenty-eight. About this time Bishop Asbury visited Canada, and appears to have been much impressed with a sense of its importance as a field of labor; and, in his estimation, Mr. Bangs was the man who should take it in charge. At the request of the bishop, Mr. Bangs consented, and was on his way to Canada when war broke out between England and the United States, which compelled him to return. His place was supplied by the Rev. Thomas Burch, who, though living in the States, was nevertheless a British subject, and he appears to have held the appointment during 1812 and the two following years. The preceding year to Mr. Burch's appointment the name of Rev. James Mitchell is found as stationed in Montreal, and the membership reported at 35 and 36. At the close of the war, Mr. Burch returned to the States, being a member of the New York Conference. After this, the work in Lower Canada was taken up by the British Conference, and the Rev

ST. JAMES STREET METHODIST CHURCH.

John Strong was appointed to Montreal. His appointment covered the years 1815 and 1816, and the membership rose to fifty-six. The next preachers were the Rev. James Booth, and the Rev. Richard Pope, who had a membership of sixty-seven. The reason that two preachers were down for Montreal was to allow one to make missionary excursions through some of the Eastern townships. In the years 1818 and 1819, the Rev. Robert Lusher came to Montreal—Mr. Booth having gone to Kingston, and Mr. Pope to St. Armand's.

At this time, or just after the war, a difficulty occurred between the English and American ministers about the use of the church in Montreal. On this subject, we have an extract of a letter from the Missionary Committee, London, to Bishop Asbury. It is as follows: "In consequence of an application made to the British Conference from the Society in Montreal, a missionary was sent to the place, and received as the Messenger of the Gospel of Peace; but we are sorry to learn that some misunderstanding has taken place between Brothers Strong, Williams, and the Presiding Elder, Ryan, for Lower Canada. From the former we have received a statement of the proceedings, and from the latter a letter of complaint. We have also received a letter from Brother Bennet, chairman of the Nova Scotia District, who has visited Montreal, and reported to us his proceedings. Upon a review of the whole, and from the most serious and deliberate consideration, we are led to conclude that, considering the relative situation of the inhabitants of Montreal, and of Canada to this country, and, particularly as a principal part of the people appear to be in favor of our missionaries, it would be for their peace and comfort, and the furtherance of the Gospel, for our friends to occupy these stations, especially Montreal, to which we conceive we have a claim; as a considerable part of money for the building of the chapel and mission house was raised in this country (England). We trust our American brethren will see the propriety of complying with our wishes, with respect to those places" (Montreal and Quebec), "not to mention their political relation to this country, which is not of little importance; for we are conscious that their habits and prejudices are in favor of English preachers, being more congenial to their views and feelings, which, certainly, should be consulted; and will tend to facilitate the success of the Gospel, and their spiritual prosperity. As you have kindly invited our esteemed brethren, Messrs Black and Bennet, to take a seat in your Conference, we have directed them to pay you a visit at Baltimore for this purpose, and to amicably arrange and settle the business, whom we trust you will receive as our representatives.

(Signed) "JAMES WOOD,
"JOSEPH BENSON,
"JAMES BUCKLEY."

The two representatives, Messrs. Black and Bennet, of Nova Scotia, did attend the American Conference at Baltimore, in May, 1816, but were unable to effect a satisfactory settlement of the difficulty, consequently, a separation took place, which continued for four years, when Bishop Emory was appointed delegate to the British Conference to adjust the difficulties concerning Canada. The result of this mission was, that Upper Canada was left under the management of the American Conference, and the Wesleyan Missions in the Lower Provinces under that of the missionaries from England.

The membership of the church in Montreal during the two years of Mr. Lusher's incumbency was 80 and 95. In the latter one of those years (1819), the first Missionary Society, auxiliary to that of the parent Society in London, England, was held. Mr. Lusher's report of this, to the committee in London, throws some interesting light upon the state of the Society, and of the lack of ministerial aid in Upper Canada.

He says: "I have the honor to inform you that the first anniversary meeting of the Auxiliary Missionary Society, formed in this city last year, was held on Monday, the 1st instant (May), in the Presbyterian Church (old St. Gabriel Street), the use of which had been kindly and cheerfully granted for the occasion (our own chapel in St. Joseph Street being too small). The preparatory sermons were preached by the Rev. John Hick, of Quebec, who was called to the chair at the general meeting. Being the only institution of the kind in the city, it excited great interest, and the meetings were numerously attended. Twenty-two pounds were collected on the Sunday evening, which, with the annual subscriptions, when received, will, I expect, amount to considerably more than the sum remitted last year. Our Treasurer, Daniel Fisher, Esq., will remit you as soon as possible. I am happy to assure you, that our cause never wore so pleasing and encouraging an aspect in this city before. The work of God is spreading : we have prayer meetings in various parts of the city, and they are found by many to be solemn and refreshing seasons. We have nearly forty prayer leaders actively engaged. The Society is also increasing and growing in grace; upon the whole, I feel greatly encouraged in my work. My dear brethren in the Upper Provinces, and in the country circuits in the Lower Province, are greatly in want of help; their field of exertion is far too large for them to cultivate without additional laborers. O, that we had more missionaries! May the Lord incline and enable you to send some more soon."

The formation of this Auxiliary Society in Montreal was followed speedily in the Upper Province. The following extract from a letter by the Rev. Thomas Catterick, dated Johnstown, Upper Canada, 25th February, 1820, attests the fact :—

"On Christmas day," writes Mr. Catterick, " we held a public meeting in the chapel at Matilda, for the purpose of forming a Missionary Meeting (or Society) to co-operate with that already formed in Montreal. The meeting was largely attended. After stating the object and design of the meeting, Mr. Wester was called to the chair, and he stated the necessity of Christians of all denominations uniting their efforts in support of Christian Missions. After pointing out the destitute state of many places, even in the Provinces, with regard to the means of religious instruction when the British missionaries first arrived, he urged, by a number of reasons, the necessity of all coming forward to assist in so good a cause. Collections were taken up amounting to £25. Collectors were appointed for the year, and the best of feeling prevailed."

From these extracts it appears that those meetings were the commencement of missionary societies throughout the two provinces. They also prove that our missionaries were needed, and that the American brethren were unable to supply the required number of preachers.

It will also have been noticed from Mr. Lusher's letter to the committee, that the little chapel (church) in St. Joseph Street, was not sufficiently large to meet the wants of the congregation. Therefore, we are not surprised that steps were taken to build a larger one. We have a minute of the trustees, recorded by them, to the following effect : "At a meeting of the committee, held Nov. 30, 1819, it was resolved : 1st. That the necessity and expediency of building a new and large chapel appears so obvious to this meeting, that measures be immediately taken for carrying the design into execution. Resolved, 2nd. That the chapel and chapel-house, which we now occupy, be sold in order to the erection of a new and larger one." Again :

"Dec. 7th, 1819. Resolved, 1st, That the lot opposite the Montreal Bank, the property of Mr. H. Gates, be purchased at £1,350. Resolved, 2nd, That Mr. John Torrance be requested to act as Treasurer, and Mr. Daniel Fisher as Secretary." This led to the erection of the *first* St. James Street Church, which was opened in 1821, when Mr. Lusher, who had been in Quebec the preceding year, returned to Montreal, where he continued for the three following years, *i. e.*, from 1821 to that of 1823 inclusive. Mr. John Hick appears as the minister for 1820, where he labored for three years, and then returned to England. The membership in 1820 was 122 ; in 1821, 119 ; in 1822, 161, and in 1823, it fell to 120.

ST. JAMES STREET METHODIST CHURCH.

The first St. James Street Church was built in the Grecian Doric order, and calculated to seat 1,200 persons. It was planned, and superintended during its erection, by the late John Try, Esq., who, in addition to giving his services free, contributed to it £100. The total cost of the church was: The ground, £1,350; building, £3,200. Total, £4,550.

The sale of the church in St. Joseph's Street brought £1,000, and the subscriptions to the new one were over £1,200, which left a debt, as will be seen, of £2,350.

This amount was advanced by Mr. John Torrance and Mr. Daniel Fisher, less a loan of £500 from Mr. McGinnis, also a member of the church.

It may here be stated that it was, in a great measure, owing to the exertions of Mr. Fisher, and his connections, that this church was erected. His sister, afterwards Mrs. Lunn, gave, in the first instance, a subscription towards its erection, of £300, and then subsequently contributed towards the liquidation of its debt. Mr. Fisher took a very active part in its management, and often paid out monies for work done at the church without making any charge for the outlay; observing, as his reason for doing so, that the debt on the church was already too large.

A painful providence closed the earthly course of this excellent man. It was through the explosion of a cask of damaged gunpowder which he had in his warehouse, and to a portion of which he had applied a lighted paper, not supposing it under the circumstances, inflammable. Thus, mysteriously, by an inadvertence surprising in a man so prudent and thoughtful in all his conduct, as Mr. Fisher was known to be, a valuable life was lost to his family, to the Church, and to the world. The Rev. Robert Alder, then the minister of the church, preached his funeral sermon, from which the following extracts are taken:

The text was Acts xi. 24: "He was a good man." "He was," said the preacher, "suddenly, unexpectedly, and in the prime of life, cut off from his family and friends, and this church loses a devoted friend; and his wife and children, an affectionate husband and father.

"Mr. Fisher was no bigot, as you well know, but was attached from principle to the Wesleyan body; and this church furnishes a splendid proof of his regard, as well for the interests of religion in general, as for the connection to which it belongs. It is well known that he was one of the original movers for its erection; but it is not generally known that he erected its elegant portico at his own expense, and in addition, advanced nearly seven hundred pounds towards the completion of the building, and for which he received no interest; and that, in compliance with his own intention, and the intentions of his widow, both principal and interest have been given up. While this chapel stands, no other monument will be necessary to perpetuate the benevolence of Daniel Fisher. His general remark was, 'The more I give, the more I receive.'"

At a meeting of the trustees, held in the St. James Street Church, 2nd March, 1827, we find the following resolution: "That the Rev. Mr. Alder be requested to draw up an inscription for a tablet, to the memory of the late Daniel Fisher, and that Mr. John Torrance is requested to procure from England a neat and handsome tablet, to be put up in the chapel." The Rev. Mr. Alder, having left Montreal shortly after the passing of the above resolution, the Rev. William Squire was requested to perform this service. This he did, and the following was inscribed on a tablet that was set up in the church:

"*Sacred to the Memory of the late*
"DANIEL FISHER, ESQ.,

"Merchant of this city, and one of the trustees of this chapel, towards the erection of which he was a munificent contributor. The inflexible integrity which marked his mercantile transactions, and the exemplary manner in which he discharged his benefactions to the indigent, were the fruits of that religion, under the influence of which, in his last afflictions, he was patient, and in death, victorious He died December 15th, 1826 in the thirty-ninth year of his age. The trustees have erected this monument as a tribute of respect to departed worth."

Mr. Fisher was a grandson of Philip Embury, who introduced Methodism into New York, and founded the first society there; and through whose exertions, in a great measure, the first Methodist chapel in New York was built. It was built in John Street, and in the year 1768. He was a trustee and the treasurer of this church. God blessed his ministry in it, and he occupied its pulpit until the arrival of Messrs. Boardman and Pilmore, Mr. Wesley's first missionaries to America.

In 1770, Mr. Embury moved, with his family, to Salem, in Washington County. Here, and in its neighborhood, he formed classes, and to him belongs the honor of having organized the first Methodist society north of New York. In 1773, after a few days' illness, from an attack of pleurisy, he died, rejoicing and triumphing in the Gospel faith he had successfully preached to others. His remains were removed in 1832 to Ashgrove, where several other distinguished ministers are buried. A large assembly attended on the occasion, who were addressed by several ministers; one of them, a countryman of the deceased, closed an eloquent address by saying, "Let me die the death that I may wear the crown of Embury. Let me live the life that I may win the spirit-watched grave of my departed countryman."

A neat, plain and appropriate marble monument, marks the spot of Embury's last resting place. There is also a handsome church built in Ashgrove, called "Embury's Church," in which an appropriate tablet, bearing an inscription to his memory, is placed.

On the breaking out of the revolutionary war, the widow Embury and her four children, with several other friends, came to Canada. She was a most exemplary woman, and died in 1833, aged seventy-three years. The Rev. Mr. Squire improved the event of her death, by preaching from Job v. 26: "Thou shalt come to thy grave in a full age, like as a shock of corn cometh in its season." Her daughter, Catherine Elizabeth, afterwards Mrs. Fisher, sen., brought up a large family in Montreal, several of whom have occupied prominent positions in the Church ; and to her careful training their success may be largely attributed. She has left numerous descendants in Canada, and a great-grandson is now (1887) filling the responsible position of trustee steward and recording steward of the St. James Street Church.

Going back to the order of ministerial succession, from which, for a while, we have been drawn, we find that, after Mr. Lusher, Mr. Henry Pope stands for Montreal for the years 1824 and 1825, when the membership was 151, and then fell to 121. In 1826, Mr. (afterwards Dr.) Robert Alder came, and left at the end of one year. He was followed by the Rev. Joseph (afterwards Dr.) Stinson, who also labored but for a single year. The probable reason for the shortness of his sojourn in Montreal was, that having now completed his period of probation, he returned to England to marry Miss Chettle, to whom he had become affianced previous to leaving England.

The next appointment to Montreal is that of the Rev. John Hick, in 1820, who had been here before, but only for one year. He now became the incumbent for three years, viz., those of 1828, 1829 and 1830. During those years the membership was at 150, 155 and 156. At the expiration of his term in Montreal, Mr. Hick removed to Stanstead, where, after two years, he was appointed to Quebec once more, and in which place, the following year, he was smitten by the fearful cholera, and after a few hours' illness, passed away in peace to his rest in heaven. Mr. Hick was an amiable man, and a very attractive and impressive preacher. He was taken away in the forty-seventh year of his age, and the twentieth of his ministry.

The Rev. Joseph Stinson, who preceded Mr. Hick in Montreal, was, after his marriage, sent to the important station of Gibraltar, where he labored with considerable success for three years. He returned to Canada in 1833, as General Superintendent of Missions, in which relation to our work he continued until 1841,

ST. JAMES STREET METHODIST CHURCH. 27

when he again returned to England. In 1858 he was reappointed to Canada, and became the President of the Canada Conference, and travelled throughout the connexion in the service of the Church. The obituary for him, in the Minutes of the Conference for 1863, supplies the following: "His well-cultivated mind and expressive language rendered him a welcome visitor to the pulpit and platform. He had a good constitution, which he devoted to his beloved Master. He seldom was ever heard to complain, notwithstanding a growing indisposition. His indomitable energy enabled him to keep his engagements until January, 1862, when, compelled by a severe internal illness, he gave up. His days of suffering were accompanied by holy communications, which took away the fear of death, and gave him a joyous assurance of eternal life. He died in Toronto, August 26th, 1862, in the fortieth year of his ministry, and the sixty-first of his life." His Montreal friends erected over his grave, in Toronto, a handsome marble monument, enclosed within a neat iron railing.

In 1827 a small chapel and school-house were erected in Gain Street, Quebec suburbs, to meet the wants of a small society, which had been formed in that neighborhood the previous year. At the end of ten years this building, owing to the growth of the congregation, was found to be too small, therefore Mr. Ferrier fitted up a neat and commodious place of worship which he presented to the Society. The following reference to it is found in the Trustees' Book. The record is dated Oct. 24th, 1837: "Resolved,—That we cheerfully accept the charge of the building in the Quebec suburbs, so generously fitted up by Mr. Ferrier, at his own expense, for the public worship of God, and that the thanks of this meeting are hereby tendered to Mr. Ferrier for his kind and liberal offer." This place was occupied by the Society, free of expense, until 1846, when the present church in Lagauchetiere Street was erected. In reference to Mr. (now the Honorable) James Ferrier, Mr. John Mathewson, from whose notes the greater part of this narrative is taken, observes: "In connection with the remarks on Mr. Ferrier's liberality towards this congregation, I cannot omit to state that he has ever been a most liberal supporter of Methodism in Montreal, contributing largely towards the erection and liquidation of the debts of the present churches. Zealous and indefatigable in his labors as Trustee, Steward, Leader, and Superintendent of the Sunday-school." And to the above it should be added, that for the extension and establishment of the Redeemer's kingdom, not only through the Methodist Church, mainly, but through other Christian organizations as well, Mr. Ferrier has ever shown himself to be a generous and a catholic sympathizer, and that in the most practical form of its expression.

In the years 1831 and 1832, the Rev. William Squire was the minister of the Methodist Church in Montreal. The latter year, owing to the breaking out of the cholera, the ground was prepared for a gracious and widespread revival of religion. The faithful and zealous spirit, which ever marked the ministry of Mr. Squire, was sure to lay hold of such an opportunity for pressing home upon the large and deeply serious congregations which attended his ministry the great and important truths of his Gospel. Several hundreds—some say, four—were at that time brought to realize the converting power of the grace of God: though that number does not appear then to have been added to the Methodist Church of Montreal. The number reported for the years of Mr. Squire's ministry are 172 and 187.

The ministers in charge for the years 1833 and 1834 were the Rev. Wm. Croscombe and Rev. Mr. Barry, and the membership is reported for these years at 350 and 395.

As the result of this revival, a society was formed in Griffintown, and in 1833 a chapel was erected on Wellington Street, which was opened for divine service in January of the following year. The services on the occasion were conducted by the Rev. Messrs. Croscombe, Squire and Barry. This branch of the St. James Street Church prospered very encouragingly, and in 1836 a day school was opened in its basement, and was carried on under the supervision of Messrs. John Mathewson, Quinn,

Howell and Ash. This school, although its course was very satisfactory, because of the financial pressure which it occasioned, had to be closed. Its closing was a matter of regret, but the expense of continuing it was more than the friends, with their other liabilities for the church, could well bear.

In the year 1835 the Rev. Wm. Lord and the Rev. Matthew Richey were appointed to Montreal. The membership rose this year to 405.

The Rev. Mr. Lord came from England to fill the chair of the Lower Canada District, and the presidential chair of the Upper Canada Conference, as two years previously a union of that Conference with the one of England had been effected. The Rev. Mr. Lord's stay in Canada was but for a year, at the expiration of which he returned to England. It is supposed that some misunderstanding with the Missionary Committee in London, in reference to certain pecuniary obligations which Mr. Lord had assumed for Victoria College—then known as the Upper Canada Academy—was the principal reason of this. Mr. (subsequently Dr.) Richey's stay in Montreal was equally brief, for at the end of the year he was led to accept the principalship of Upper Canada Academy, which position he held for the three years following.

In the year 1836 the Rev. William M. Harvard and the Rev. I. B. Selley arrived from England; sent by the Missionary Committee, London, and took up their residence in Montreal. They were its appointed ministerial supply. Mr. Harvard's appointment was similar to that of Mr. Lord's; and he therefore, as did his predecessor, presided not only over the Lower Canada District but over the Upper Canada Conference as well. This year the membership in Montreal was 560; showing that a very steady and marked success attended the ministry of God's servants here * The following year another change took place, and the Rev. Robert L. Lusher again took charge of Montreal,

* Mr. Harvard was one of the companions of Dr. Coke on his first journey to Continental India.

after an absence of eighteen years, which he spent in several of the principal stations and circuits in England. Mr. Lusher had as his colleague the Rev. Edmund Botterell, who also was from England. The membership of this year is given at 585.

Mr. Lusher continued in Montreal, as the superintendent minister, for three years, and had as his colleague, after Mr. Botterell, the Rev. R. Hutchinson, and then the Rev. John P. Hetherington. About this time, Mr. Lusher was seized with paralysis, which eventually compelled him to retire from the active services of the ministry. Nevertheless, after finishing his three years in Montreal, he ministered to the little church in Three Rivers for two years more, when his complete retirement was necessitated. Seven years after this, the 18th July, 1849, Mr. Lusher died. This was the sixty-second of his age, and the thirty-second of his ministry. Mr. Lusher was a man of amiable and gentlemanly bearing. He was a faithful and effective preacher of the Gospel, both in word and life; and his memory is revered by those who had his acquaintance. The membership during these years was 585, 510 and 420. The great many removals which are constantly going on from the principal cities and towns of Canada, will doubtless account for the remarkable fluctuations which these figures show. This fact is ofttimes felt to be of a depressing nature, by the ministerial laborers especially; and yet there is the relieving assurance, that if, by such removals, their charge in one place is weakened and reduced, others are strengthened and enriched by them; and, therefore, the cause of Christ, as a whole, is not a loser thereby.

The year 1840, the Rev. William Squire is again found in Montreal, occupying its leading ministerial position, aided by the Rev. Mr. Hetherington. Mr. Lusher's name appears also, but it is simply as a superannuated minister. The membership, this year, seems to have fallen lower than it had been for several years previously. It now is reported at 384.

The following year, 1841, is marked by another change. The Rev. Mr. Hetherington was removed to Toronto West, and the

ST. JAMES STREET METHODIST CHURCH.

Rev. John Borland was appointed as his successor, and Mr. Squire's colleague. The membership in this year was 412. During the winter of this year, revival services were held in the Wellington Street Church, which resulted in the conversion of some fifty persons. The following year the health of Mr. Borland gave way, through a severe cold he had contracted, and which threatened a fatal termination. The symptoms became aggravated, from the fact that he continued to prosecute his labors while taking prescribed remedies. The consequence was, it became a decided and severe case of bronchitis, which compelled his retirement, for the remainder of the year from all labor, and removal from the city. At the instance of a friend, who had a ship loading at Quebec for Liverpool, England, and who kindly urged upon him the acceptance of a passage in her when she left, Mr. Borland, on consulting his friends, was induced to accept the generous offer of James Carson, Esq., of Dublin, and left for England in August of that year. He was kindly taken by the Missionary Committee in London, and abode with Dr. Alder until the following spring, when he returned to Canada and to his work in the Church, thoroughly renewed in health, and very much profited, in every way, by his stay in the great city of London for nearly five months. During the absence of Mr. Borland, Mr. Squire had supplies from several of the ministerial brethren around him, so that, through this aid, and his own systematic, earnest, and effective labors, the work of the Lord was fully sustained. Mr. Borland returned from England to Montreal in time to wind up the year with his Superintendent, and then remove with him to Quebec, where they were both appointed for the coming year, and where they continued together very successfully for the two years following.

Before leaving Montreal, the Quarterly Meeting passed the following resolution in reference to Mr. Squire, of which he was in every way most deserving : "That this meeting cannot allow the tie that unites pastor and people to be severed by the approaching departure of our valuable Superintendent, Rev. William

Squire, without recording its deep sense of the great service which he has rendered the cause of religion, in this circuit, by his untiring zeal and assiduity ; and also the high respect which it entertains for him as an able minister of the New Testament." The last year of Mr. Squire's ministry in Montreal was signalized by a remarkable revival of religion, which added many valuable members to the Church.

The following year, 1843, the ministers for Montreal were, the Rev. Matthew Lang, Rev. John B. Brownell and the Rev. Robert Cooney, and a membership of 566 is given.

Mr. Lang had, before coming to Montreal, been for twenty years laboring in the Provinces, mainly that of Lower Canada. He came to Montreal from Quebec, where he had been for the two preceding years. Mr. Brownell had, previous to his coming to Canada, labored not only in England, but in the West India Islands, and for four years on the Island of Malta. In Canada he had, for four years, previous to his coming to Montreal, ministered on the Dunham Circuit. Mr. Cooney was originally a Roman Catholic. He was converted in Nova Scotia, and there entered the work of our ministry. His first appointment was Prince Edward Island, in 1831. He came up to the Province of Quebec, in 1838, and was stationed at Odelltown. Here he was, for a time, in the very midst of the rebellion, which had broken out the previous year, in the Upper and Lower Provinces of Canada. The road on which he resided was a highway by which the rebels moved for their invasion of Canada from the States— where many from Canada had gone, and being joined by others in the States, they organized themselves into a force to march into Canada, their destination being Montreal. Their line of march was through Odelltown ; and here the loyalists of the place rallied and planned a defence to resist their progress The church was taken—being strongly built of stone—by the men of the place, as their fort, and from which they deployed to attack the approaching rebels. A battle was fought, in which several of both sides were killed and wounded, but the rebels were forced to retire, and their plans were frustrated. Marks of the battle were observable, for many years, in several parts of the church, which attested its militant character in other ways than those strictly spiritual.

After two years these brethren were removed, and succeeded by Rev. Dr. Richey, the Rev. Charles Churchill, and the Rev. George H. Davis. The membership had now risen to the respectable number of 720. Dr. Richey was a man in every way remarkable; majestic in bearing, elegant in manners, and was undoubtedly one of the most eloquent ministers of his day. After sustaining the principalship of the Upper Canada Academy—now Victoria College—for three years, he went to Toronto, and then to Kingston, and in each place spent other three years, so that nine years had elapsed between his first, and now his second, appointment to Montreal. Mr. Churchill came from England to Halifax in 1837, which was his first year in the ministry. He continued in the Nova Scotia District until 1844, when he came to St. John's, in the Quebec District, and remained for one year.

The Rev. Mr. Davis, the junior colleague, entered the ministry in England, in 1842, and for two years had the educational advantages of the Richmond Institute, near London. His first appointment in the regular work of the ministry was Montreal, in the year 1845. Mr. Davis has continued to labor in Canada until lately; having finished his fortieth year in the active work, he was compelled, through bodily infirmity, to ask a superannuated relation to the Conference, and resides now in Montreal. The membership reported these years of 1845, 1846 and 1847, was 770, 803 and 883.

In the first year of the incumbency of these ministers, the present St James Street Church was finished. The opening services, with other points of interest, were given by the Montreal *Herald*, as follows :—

"DEDICATION OF THE NEW WESLEYAN CHURCH, GREAT ST. JAMES STREET, MONTREAL.

"The 27th July, 1845, will long be remembered, in Montreal, by the British Wesleyans, as the commencement of a new era in the history of Methodism in this city. On this day, the large and elegant building in Great St. James Street was solemnly dedicated to the worship of Almighty God. According to this time, it may indeed be said, 'What hath God wrought!' A grateful recollection of God's goodness in the past leads us in reflection to the time when, in the year 1808, the first Methodist chapel, now used as the Exchange, in St. Joseph Street, was built, the Society numbering then only twenty or thirty individuals, supplied ministerially by British missionaries, who continued their efforts until increasing numbers warranted the erection of what was then considered a very large edifice in the same street, now occupied by the new and spacious church.

"Notwithstanding the erection of the first St. James Street Church, and, twelve or thirteen years afterwards, of one in Wellington Street, and another in the Quebec suburbs, yet considerable inconvenience was felt in the central church for enlarged accommodation for those who sought an opportunity of worshipping there. Hence this new and much larger church was built. Its size was $111\frac{1}{2}$ feet by 73 feet, and capable of seating nearly two thousand persons. It has been known to have within its walls, on many special occasions, three thousand of a congregation. Its cost was sixty thousand dollars.

"The opening sermons," we are told by the *Herald*, "were preached (at the request of the trustees) by their own ministers. The Rev. Matthew Richey, A.M., preached on the Sabbath morning, and the Rev. Mr. Churchill in the evening. The Rev. Dr. Carruthers, Congregationalist, preached in the afternoon, and the Rev. Dr. Wilkes on a week evening. On all the occasions the congregations were extremely large; in the morning, especially, the place was crowded, with not less than three thousand persons, many hundreds going away, unable to obtain entrance, or a seat. A delightful, hallowed influence prevailed during the whole services; and the effects, we trust, will be felt for a long time to come. The collections taken up amounted to $437.57.

"There were several circumstances connected with the opening services which served to heighten the satisfaction enjoyed by the trustees. His Excellency Lord Metcalfe, the Governor-General, attended the morning service, accompanied by his private secretary and aide-de-camp. His Excellency was pleased to express his admiration of the edifice itself, and his satisfaction with the services as then conducted. The Rev. R. L. Lusher, under whose superintendence the former chapel was built and dedicated, twenty-four years ago, was also present, though in a state of great debility; and several ministers of other denominations attended, assisting in the services, and adding to the general interest of the dedication."

The *Times*, another of the city papers, gives a glowing account of the opening occasion, from which I quote the following simply: "The ceremony of the dedication of the Wesleyan Church took place on Sunday morning, at half-past ten o'clock. The church was filled—in fact, many persons were unable to obtain admission. His Excellency the Governor-General, attended by his staff, was present. The Rev. Matthew Richey, A.M., preached from the text—Ephesians v. 25-27—beginning, 'As Christ also loved the Church.' The reverend gentleman was most eloquent—in fact, he is one of those pulpit orators, so simple and fervent, yet withal so powerful, that he never speaks without impressing his truths on the minds of his hearers."

Immediately on the completion of the Great St. James Street Church, two others were commenced, one in Lagauchetiere (now Palace Street East), and the other in Ottawa Street, the west, or Griffintown portion of the city. They both were built and opened during the incumbency of Messrs. Richey, Churchill and

Davis; in each instance Mr. (now Dr.) Richey preaching the opening sermon.

The next ministerial appointments for Montreal were those of the Rev. John Jenkins, Rev. Charles DeWolfe, and the Rev. Lachlin Taylor. Mr. (subsequently Dr.) Jenkins entered the ministry in England in 1835, and after spending two years in the Theological Institution, was sent out as missionary to Goobee, in India. Here he labored for three years, and then removed to Bangalore, where he continued for two years; and owing to failing health, he was removed to Malta. After two years on the Island, he returned to England. Three years subsequently, at the instance of the Missionary Committee, he came to Montreal. Here he remained six years, after which he removed to Philadelphia.

The Rev. Charles DeWolfe was a native of Nova Scotia. His first profession was that of law, but which he soon resigned for the more congenial one of preaching the Gospel. This took place in 1837, and after occupying several of the principal stations in Prince Edward Island and Nova Scotia, he came to Montreal in 1848. Here he remained, highly respected, for three years, and then went to Quebec. Failure in health compelled him to resign this station for the comparatively light one of Three Rivers, when, after three years, he returned to his native Province. For genial manners and grace, and finish as a preacher, he had few, if any, equals.

The Rev. Lachlin (subsequently Dr.) Taylor was the third appointee to Montreal. He remained in it, however, but one year, and then removed to Three Rivers. From this, at the end of the year, he returned to Upper Canada, and became the agent for the Bible Society in that Province. Here he continued to labor with much effectiveness for about six years, when he became, and for a similar period served the Church as, one of its missionary secretaries

Several important events took place in the Church in Montreal anterior to those just referred to. One of these was the

ST. JAMES STREET METHODIST CHURCH. 37

introduction of means specially appointed for revival services. Hitherto the ordinary means, used at the stated times, were those on which dependence was placed for effecting the conversion of sinners and the growth of spiritual life of believers. But the extraordinary means, forced, as it were, upon the Church during the cholera visitation of 1832, and the wonderful results which attended them, induced the conviction that such means should be of frequent use at suitable times. Early in the year 1833, the Rev. Wm. Croscombe, then stationed in Montreal, engaged in a series of such services, assisted by the Rev. Mr. Lang, of St. Armand, and the Rev. Mr. Little, of St. Albans, of the Vermont Conference. At Mr. Little's suggestion, who was compelled to return to his own work, application was made to the Rev. James Caughey, then stationed at Burlington, to come to Montreal and aid our brethren in their work, which was developing most encouragingly. Mr. Caughey complied with the request and came, and soon showed that he possessed extraordinary qualities of mind and heart as an evangelist. This was a turning point in this distinguished man's life; for immediately afterwards he changed his pastoral ministry for that of a revivalist, in which for a number of years he has labored in the principal cities and towns in Canada, in many of the States of the Union, and as well in several of those in England and Ireland. He success as a laborer in this department of Christian effort is shown in the conversion to God of many hundreds of persons, and in urging on of believers to the higher attainments of the Christian life,— of the possibilities of which he was himself a notable example. The ministry of Mr. Caughey was remarkable for simplicity of diction, aptness of illustration, point and force of application, and great spiritual unction, the consequence of which was immense congregations to attend his ministry, and the conversion to God of hundreds, if not thousands, of his fellowmen.

After several weeks of labor in Montreal at the time indicated, Mr. Lang and Mr. Caughey went down to Quebec to aid our Church there, who were engaged in similar revival services.

The Rev. Mr. Tomkins, the minister in charge, had succeeded the Rev. Mr. Hick, who, in the early part of the year, had died from cholera, was with the aid of his official members, engaged in special revival work. The coming of these distinguished ministers was heartily welcomed, and the effect of their labors was truly marvellous. The old city of Quebec was strangely moved, and many, even Roman Catholics, who had never before been in a Methodist place of worship, came to hear and see for themselves the things that were everywhere reported to be taking place. Since then Mr. Caughey has several times visited and labored in the cities of Montreal and Quebec, and in each instance with striking effect, and most desirable consequences. After years of evangelistic labors of this kind, he is now (1887), and has been for several years past, as the result of weakness and bodily infirmity, retired from his greatly-loved and useful labors, in a town in the State of New Jersey, where he awaits the call of his Lord and Master to his home in the skies.

Another event in which the Church in Montreal felt a deep and lively interest was that of the union of the Upper Canada Conference with the parent Conference in England. Several circumstances of moment had called the attention of the Missionary Committee of London to a Mission among the Indians of Upper Canada, and the occupancy of a distinct position from that of the Upper Canada Conference, in the cities of Kingston and Toronto. A considerable objection to this movement was felt by our Upper Canada brethren; and the best way of meeting the difficulty and of preventing the evils which it was supposed would arise from the dual residence and labors of Methodistic agents in this Province, was a union of the two bodies. This was effected in 1833.

From various causes, however, the union was not lasting, nor had it been harmonious. Upper Canada Methodism had originated by missionaries from the States, and for several years was not only identified with the body there, but was superintended

ST. JAMES STREET METHODIST CHURCH. 39

by officials receiving their appointment there. This gave rise to the idea that the Methodist Church of Upper Canada was an alien body, a feeling fostered by the High Church party in the provinces. To neutralize an impression which was unjust to the great bulk of the ministers and members of the Church, who were as much Canadians and loyal to the British throne as were their maligners, the Church sought and obtained a separation from, and independence to, the American body. Still they were stigmatized as Republicans, and opposed to a monarchical form of government. The Church party the more zealously spread this libel against the Upper Canada Methodists, because they through their organ, the *Christian Guardian*, but recently started, vigorously opposed their exclusive assumptions, and effectively disposed of their unjust pretensions. This work of self-defence necessarily brought them in line, in several particulars, with certain prominent and extreme men in political matters—a fact the High Church party made use of for their ends. These circumstances had a prejudicial influence upon the minds of the English Methodists at home, and in several parts of Canada; and they looked, as a consequence, with much doubtfulness upon a union of the bodies, unless in a way that would thoroughly Anglify the Methodism of Canada.

At a meeting of the Trustees, Stewards, and Leaders of the St. James Street Church, April the 8th, 1834, at which this subject was discussed, the Rev. William Croscombe presiding, assisted by the Rev. John Barry, the following resolutions were passed. A preamble to them is given in these words :—

"It was deemed of vital importance to the interests of British Wesleyan Methodism, in the Provinces of Upper and Lower Canada, relative to the union question, on which the meeting had previously expressed its opinion, to ascertain the particular views of every member of the meeting, upon what terms they, in their judgment, would consider it safe and honorable for the British Wesleyan Methodist Societies in these provinces to enter into an union with the Methodist Episcopal Church of Upper Canada, when we, the undersigned, unanimously agreed to adopt and abide by the following resolutions :

"First,—That in order to effect and settle the union, at present attempted between the British Wesleyan Methodist Societies in these provinces, and the Canadian Episcopal Methodist Societies, there must be an unreserved renunciation of the Episcopal system, and a cordial and unqualified adoption of the doctrines, discipline, institutions and usages of British Wesleyan Methodism.

"Secondly,—That until the spirit of the above resolution be fully demonstrated by the cordial reception of British Wesleyan Methodism amongst the present Episcopal Methodist Societies in the Upper Province, this Society must conscientiously refuse to be included in the terms of the Union. Signed by the Trustees, with one exception, he being absent, and sixteen Leaders."

Again, we have a record of a "special meeting of the Trustees and Leaders, called at the request of the Rev. Mr. Alder, Rev. Wm. Croscombe in the chair."

"Rev. Mr. Alder again went into the Union question, and now fully and minutely explained the object the British Wesleyan Missionary Committee had in view when they first entered into negotiation upon the subject, which explanation was deemed satisfactory to the meeting; viz., that the object of the British Wesleyan Missionary Committee, in forming the union with the Episcopal Methodists of the Upper Province, was in order to improve the general character of Methodism amongst them, and to bring their system in unison with that of the British Wesleyan Connexion."

It is added that "a copy of the above resolutions was furnished to Dr. Alder at the time."

The union was formed, but owing to circumstances it is not desirable here to enlarge upon, was of short duration. At the end of seven years a separation, under the most painful circumstances, was brought about, and for six years bitter fruits from the disruption grew up in a number of places. Healing and

ST. JAMES STREET METHODIST CHURCH. 41

uniting influences were again applied, and in 1847 a reunion was effected, which has grown until at length it has gathered into its fold the Methodism of the whole of Canada, Newfoundland, and the Island of Bermuda, and to-day (1888) is one of the most compact, harmonious, and effective members of the great Methodist family of the world.

In the year 1854, the Methodism of Montreal was divided into three Circuits, and became known as Montreal Centre, Montreal East, and Montreal West. The churches had for several years their separate leaders' meeting, but came together at their Quarterly Meeting occasions for the financial interests they had in common. Further, they had continued in the regular circuit exchange of ministers. The division caused sore trouble, having been carried out by those in authority in a very arbitrary manner, and entirely against the wishes of those directly interested. It is very hard for us, after a lapse of thirty-four years, to understand, *first*, why this division was pushed so harshly, even to the extent of driving from the Church the great majority of two whole congregations, and *secondly*, why the movement should have been so bitterly opposed; as we view things at the present day, churches situated as they were would work out their own schemes better apart than as one.

The result of this arbitrary division of the Circuit into three was the immediate withdrawal from the Eastern Church of all the official members, except one, and of 183 members out of a total number of 248; and in the Western Church, the officials with one exception all withdrew, and also the majority of the members. The greater part of the seceders united in inviting the New Connexion Methodist Church to open a work in the city, the result of which was the building of the Panet Street Church for the Eastern section, and of the Dupre Lane Church for the Western branch.

The result to St. James Street Society was very embarrassing. As the Griffintown and Quebec suburbs churches both belonged to their trust, it followed that if the revenue from these Societies fell off, and did not equal the expenditure, the deficiency had to be made up by them. The extent of the loss thus accruing to them may be put down as the gross amount of receipts of the two New Connexion churches, which after careful calculation, may be set down at $72,000. That is the gross revenue, including the cost of their two churches, and deducting what these buildings were sold for after the reunion in 1874.

Occupying the Centre Church we find Rev. John (subsequently Dr.) Jenkins. For three years he continued the superintendent of the three churches, having as his colleague, Mr. DeWolfe. Who the third preacher was for those two years cannot now be stated; it is probable that the supply was an irregular one.

The three following years Mr. Jenkins continued in the Centre Church, and for two of them the Rev. G. N. A. F. T. Dickson, recently from New Brunswick, although a native of Ireland, and just then received into our ministry, was appointed to the Eastern Church; and the Rev. Mr. Squire took charge of the Western Church, and here it was that this devoted and successful minister of Christ finished his course and entered into rest. And yet in his death there is a mournful impression that it was a sacrifice to the demand of an over-scrupulous conscience. Mr. Squire had attended a western merchant, Mr. Young, brother to Rev. William Young, one of our Upper Canada ministers, who had come to Montreal on business and was seized by cholera. Mr. Young died, and Mr. Squire was requested to sign a certificate of his death, for his friends in the West. But Mr. Squire had not seen him die, nor was he otherwise assured, than by the declaration of the friends present and of the undertaker, that in the coffin before him was the body of the Mr. Young in question. He therefore insisted that the lid of the coffin should be removed, and that he should have ocular proof of the fact he was to certify; and this being done, he gave the required signature, sickened and went home to die. His death occurred the next morning, being Sabbath, the 17th October, 1852. His age was fifty-six, and he had been in the ministry of the Methodist Church for thirty-two

ST. JAMES STREET METHODIST CHURCH. 43

years. It will not be out of place here to remark, that his interment was the first in the Mount Royal Cemetery of our city. A worthy firstfruit to so noble a monument of the Montreal Protestant community.

The Rev. William Scott was Mr. Squire's successor in the Ottawa Street Church, and the Rev. George (now Dr.) Douglas was that of Mr. Dickson in the Eastern one.

To the District Meeting of 1853, held in Montreal, the Rev. Dr. Wood came, by the appointment of the Missionary Committee, London, and took the chair which by Mr. Squire's death had been made vacant. The subject of the union of the Lower Canada District with the Upper Canada Conference was taken up and decided upon. The reluctance hitherto felt to such a step had become very much weakened, and the ministers of this District were disposed to offer no further objection to the wish of the Committee in England and many friends of our Church in Upper Canada. The representation and counsels of the chairman, Dr. Wood, had great influence in this direction, and, as a consequence, and in promotion of the object, Messrs. Jenkins, Borland and Brock were appointed to attend the Upper Canada Conference, to be held in the city of Hamilton. The reception accorded these brethren by the Conference, and the impression made upon their minds by the intercourse they had with several of its prominent members, and what they saw of its workings during the time they attended its sessions were such, that a most cordial concurrence in the members of the District for the union was the result. The next year the union was consummated, and as a welding of it visibly and really, the Rev. Wellington Jeffers was appointed to the Centre Church, St. James Street, Montreal, the Rev. John Borland was sent up from Quebec to the Richmond Street Church, in Toronto, and the Rev. William Pollard from London, C.W., to Quebec. The membership in Montreal at this date was 880.

The Rev. Wellington (now Dr.) Jeffers continued the incumbent of the St. James Street (Centre) Church, for 1854, 1855 and 1856, during which years the membership for this church rose from 250 to 313. The Rev. John Gemley, from Toronto East, came as Dr. Jeffers' successor in 1857, and held the appointment for the three following years. One of these years, that of 1858, Mr. Gemley had as an assistant the Rev. Ebenezer Robson. The membership was 353, 376 and 366. Mr. Gemley was a man of great amiability and very general acceptance, and one who found something to do for every young man in the church. He was very highly esteemed by all the young men, both members and non-members.

Next we have the Rev. Isaac B. Howard for one year, after which he became successor to the Rev. George Young, in the Ottawa Street Church, for the next two years; and the Rev. Ephraim B. Harper (now Dr.) became his successor to the St. James Street Church. Mr. Harper had as an assistant, for one year, the Rev. Charles Lavell, M.A. The membership these years was 386, 388 and 585.

In the last year of Mr. Harper's incumbency of the Centre Church, and the first of the Rev. Henry F. Bland in the East, another movement was started for more church accommodation for the increasing numbers that were placing themselves under the Methodist ministry in the city. A notice of this movement in the Montreal *Gazette*, bearing the initials H. F. B., gives the following facts: "During the fall of 1863 the impression deepened in some minds that, in order to meet the growing wants of the city, another church extension effort should be made. In the following March this impression took practical shape, and the sum of nearly $60,000 was subscribed. The three new churches in Sherbrooke Street, Dorchester Street, and Point St. Charles, have been opened within the last year, and are the result of this effort. Including the one recently erected at St. Lamberts, there are now seven Wesleyan Methodist churches in Montreal, with a large membership, independent of adherents. Representatives of Montreal Methodism are scattered all over Western Canada, and the great prairie states beyond are not strangers to them."

ST. JAMES STREET METHODIST CHURCH.   45

Following Mr. Harper, the Rev. James Elliott, with the Rev. Mr. Lavell as his colleague, came to Montreal in 1865. The next year, the Rev. Wm. (now Dr.) Briggs succeeded Mr. Lavell, who continued as co-laborers for the following two years, which completed Mr. (now Dr.) Elliott's term. In one of these years (that of 1867) the Dominion Square Church ceased to be worked in connection with the Centre Church, and had allotted to it a separate and independent condition, Mr. Elliott retaining charge of the Centre, and Mr. Briggs that of the other, now known in the Minutes as " Montreal the Fourth." The membership of the Centre Church is set down as 431, and that of Montreal the Fourth, or Dominion Square Church, at 140.

Rev. Dr. Elliott owed his standing in the Conference to the safety of his judgment, the weight of his character, and his efficiency as a preacher. He was not a declaimer, nor critically expository, but his preaching was original, sage and satisfying.

Rev. Dr. Briggs, according to Dr. Carroll, is a man, modest without bashfulness ; as a Christian, religious without cant ; as a preacher, fervent and eloquent without rant; as a platform speaker, ready, pointed and pertinent ; and as a connexional business man, capable and successful, without being fussy and pretentious.

In 1867, Rev. George Douglas succeeded Mr. Elliott, and had as a colleague Rev. John B. Clarkson. The name of the Rev. George (now Dr.) Douglas calls for a special reference here. Dr. Douglas entered the ministry in 1848, and having spent one year on the Melbourne Mission, in the Eastern Townships, was sent to England to receive the benefit of a course of training in the Theological Institution in Richmond, near London. But, much to the disappointment of himself and friends, and for some unexplained reason, he was sent, not to the Institution, but by the Missionary Committee to their mission on the Island of Bermuda. Here he remained for somewhat less than two years, but sufficiently long to contract a disease from the malaria of the

Island, which has held to him with a terrible tenacity to the present. Its power may in some measure be apprehended when it is known that it has destroyed all sensation in his hands and feet, and, latterly, of all power of vision. It compelled him to take a supernumerary relation for a year, while it has brought upon him an amount of physical and mental suffering indescribable, and certainly incredible to any one not fully informed of all the facts of his case. And yet he has, during this time, ministered with marked efficiency and success, to the principal churches of Kingston, Toronto, Hamilton and Montreal, in all of which, with one exception, he was the superintendent minister. He has filled the offices of Chairman of his District, President of his Conference, Vice-President for one term, and President for another, of the General Conference. He has served his brethren as their delegate to the General Conference of the Methodist Church South, and the great Ecumenical Council in London; and for the last fifteen years he has held, with great acceptance and ability, the office of Principal of our Theological College in Montreal. Such a series of labors, distinguished for efficiency and success, and under the pressure of so much infirmity and suffering, is doubtless without a parallel in modern times.

In the year 1870 the Rev. John Potts came first to Montreal, and to the Centre, or St. James Street Church. The membership during the three years he ministered to it was 399, 429 and 448.

The successor of Mr. Potts was the Rev. Alexander Sutherland. The second year of Mr. Sutherland's incumbency, the Rev. Benjamin Longley, B.A., was his colleague, the membership being 516 and 487. During the second year, Mr. (now Dr.) Sutherland was called to the important and responsible office of joint Secretary with the Rev. Dr. Wood to the Missionary Society, in which office he continues to the present, highly esteemed for the distinguished ability and devotion he gives to the duties of his office. The successor of Mr. Sutherland was the Rev. Leonard Gaetz, from the Nova Scotia Conference, whose

ST. JAMES STREET METHODIST CHURCH. 47

colleague, as he had been that of Mr. Sutherland, was Mr. Longley.

Mr. Gaetz was a minister of great native eloquence, who all too soon was forced to retire from the ministry, on account of the permanent failure of his health.

The Rev. Hugh Johnston, M.A., B.D., became Mr. Gaetz's successor in 1878, 1879 and 1880; the membership being 473, 367, and 402. Mr. Johnston is genial, graceful, scholarly and devoted in his ministry, and was a great favorite with everybody. Mr. Johnston was succeeded by Rev. Delmer E. Mallory, a young man of remarkable consecration, who subsequently retired from the ministry, and became the assistant of the renowned Dr. Cullis, of Boston, in his Christian work.

At the Conference of 1882, the Rev. Dr. Potts was appointed a second time to the St. James Street Church. The Doctor was a great favorite, and popular not only with the Methodist people of the city, but with those of the other Protestant Churches as well. Hence large congregations, particularly on the Sabbath evenings, attended his ministry, while his name as a speaker on any of the more general interests of the day, was ever hailed with much satisfaction.

Following Dr. Potts, we have the Rev. John Philp, M.A. Dr. Potts returned to a former charge he had in Toronto, that of the Elm Street Church, and Mr. Philp came to Montreal from the Carlton Street Church in Toronto. Thus the interlacing and bond-strengthening influence of our itinerant system works in promoting the connexional character of our Church, and the application of the varying talents of its ministry to the equally varying tastes, susceptibilities and wants of the people.

For several years past the desirability of erecting a new church for the St. James Street congregation in a more central position had been felt. The frontal portion of the city has long been given up to business purposes, while residences have been sought for in the more remote portions; a consequence of which has been, that in this, as in other churches, the distance between the church and the dwellings of its members was becoming greater year by year, and, in not a few instances, was felt to be a real inconvenience. After much prayerful consideration, a step was taken of very considerable moment, viz., the purchase of a square fronting on St. Catherine Street. The property was known as the old Allan estate. It had passed into the hands of the Canadian Pacific Railway Company, and by them was designed as their city station. But, having abandoned the idea of placing their station in that locality, they became willing to sell the property.

Shortly after Mr. Philp's induction into the St. James Street Church, measures were taken to secure this place, and a purchase was effected. The amount demanded and paid was a high one —$70,000. Yet its size and commanding position—being a square, having a street on each of its sides, and along its front one of the leading streets of the city—show it to be quite worth the sum paid for it, and to be an important acquisition. Immediately on acquiring the site, active measures were taken for commencing the erection of a church, all of which has been so far completed that the corner-stone, in a most imposing ceremony, was laid by the Hon. James Ferrier on Saturday, the 11th June, 1887. The weather was unusually fine, and a large gathering of the friends, and of sightseers generally, witnessed the ceremony. We append the full report from the *Daily Witness* :—

"It was a pleasant, and at the same time an impressive occasion when, on Saturday afternoon, thousands of our citizens, old and young, gathered around the corner-stone of the magnificent church edifice which is now being erected at the corner of St. Catherine and City Councillors' Streets, perpetuating in the minds of future generations the liberality and loyalty of the old St. James Street congregation. There was one man present especially whose honored form called forth the respect due to these great qualities, and that was the venerable Senator James Ferrier, who, perhaps above all others, has financially contributed

ST. JAMES STREET METHODIST CHURCH. 49

to the success of the Methodist Church in the city of Montreal. It seemed particularly fitting that he should be chosen by the trustees of this latest monument to the zeal and liberality of his denomination to give official sanction to the worthy enterprise, which will be from this day carried on with uninterrupted vigor to completion and dedication.

"At three o'clock, the lot upon which the church is being built presented a most animated appearance. A large platform was erected immediately above the foundation walls and overhung by canvas, affording shelter from the sun for the clergy and laity who were to take part in the ceremonies. A great quantity of bunting, in the shape of national flags and banners, had also been suspended on every side, and nothing evidently had been left undone to distinguish the occasion as one of the brightest in Methodist history. The Rev. J. Philp, M.A., presided, and seated around him were the Rev. Dr. Shaw, President of the Montreal Conference; Rev. Mark Guy Pearse, of London, Eng.; Rev. J. Henderson, Rev. Dr. Antliff, Rev. Dr. Saunders, Rev. J. Kines, Rev. John Borland, Rev. S. Bond, Rev. Mr. Baldwin, Rev. W. Jackson; Rev. Robert Campbell, of St. Gabriel Presbyterian Church; Hon. James Ferrier, Dr. Alexander, Ald. McBride, Ald. Holland, ex-Ald. Hood, Messrs. G. H. Davis, John Torrance, John Cowan, J. Fairman, F. Fairman, Thos. Chambers, G. E. Jaques, jun., G. Young, G. Vipond, J. Ferrier, D. Graham, Robt. Miller, Wm. Hodgson, J. E. Alston, Geo. Armstrong, E. T. Wilkes, J. H. Elliott, Jas. Griffin, Thos. Burdon, Samuel Finley, Alex. Shaw, E. A. Hilton, and many others.

"The service was commenced by singing hymn 669,—

> "'This stone to Thee in faith we lay;
> To Thee this Temple, Lord, we build;
> Thy power and goodness here display,
> And be it with Thy presence filled.'

"A very fervent prayer was then offered up by the Rev. Dr. Saunders, after which the pastor of the church read from Psalm cxxxii., "Lord, remember David and all his afflictions." responded to by the congregation present. This was supplemented by a lesson from 1 Cor. iii. 9-23, read by the Rev. Mr. Jackson. The Rev. Mr. Bond announced hymn 662, which brought the strictly devotional portion of the exercises to a close.

"Mr. G. E. Jaques then stepped to the front of the platform, and in a clear voice read the lengthy and most interesting document which was soon to be consigned to the interior of the stone, and an exact copy of which paper appeared in Saturday's *Witness*.

"Before calling upon the speakers, Mr. Philp alluded feelingly to the forced absence of the Rev. Dr. Douglas, owing to pressing engagements in the West; but he sent them his blessing and his prayers, and was with them in spirit.

"The Rev. J. Henderson was the first speaker called upon, and his appropriate and eloquent address was listened to with the greatest attention. 'I suppose,' said he, 'that the Methodist people of this city look forward with a great deal of joy and hope to the completion of this great work, and, with me, are considering what influence it will probably exercise upon Methodism throughout the city, the Province, and even our great Dominion. I think that I am right in presuming that it will change the entire horoscope of Methodism over the length and breadth of our land. Senator Ferrier, in laying the corner-stone of this church, is about to plunge into our social and religious life a mighty pebble, which cannot fail to send a ripple of righteousness and truth from one end of this country to the other. When I look upon the beautiful picture of this church, I cannot help realizing that its completion will open up a new and still brighter chapter of Methodism in this city and country. I am getting old, or at least some of my friends think so, and I can remember when I had moments far from hopeful regarding the future of our Church in Montreal, surrounded and affected as she was by the powerful influences which the Church of Rome never failed to exert in all parts of the Province of Quebec. I thought at one time that the tide was certainly receding, and that we would be left hopelessly

ST. JAMES STREET METHODIST CHURCH.   51

stranded ; but now, thank God, things are changed; the tidal wave of Protestant truth is sweeping upward and onward, bringing to the Methodist branch, as to all the others, satisfaction for the work accomplished, and a greater hope for a glorious future.' The reverend gentleman then took a rapid and most eloquent retrospect of the good work and general prosperity which the different Methodist congregations of the city had achieved during the past few years, and paid a glowing tribute to the laborious zeal of the worthy pastors of St. James Street, Dominion Square, Ottawa Street, Seigneurs Street, Douglas and East End churches. He announced amid cheers, that owing to the kindness of his own people, and to the prosperity which had dawned upon them also, he was about to go back and pay a visit to his Old Scotia—the land of Bruce, of Scott, and of Burns. He would tell his friends at home—although some would not believe him—that one of the finest church edifices in Canada would soon be completed, and that it belonged to the Methodists. Referring to the sister Churches, in his eloquent peroration, the speaker said : ' I hope, if there are any of our good Presbyterian and Episcopal brothers here, that they will believe us to be actuated by the best feeling toward them all. I love the Presbyterian Church, because it is the Church of my motherland ; and I love the good old Episcopal Church because she is the mother of our own. It was said that Methodism would prove to be nothing more than a freshet of thought, taking possession of the human mind for a limited time and then receding into complete obscurity, utterly forgotten and utterly unknown ; it has, however, as your presence in such numbers shows, grandly proved to be a fixed and shining star, whose sacred nature will flash out the sparks of truth and holiness long after rush and taper lights will have ceased to exist.'

"The Rev. Dr. Antliff followed in one of those practical and fluent addresses, characteristic of the pastor of the Dominion Square Church. He said that he could heartily join in the wish, which had found universal expression that day, that the influence for good and the work accomplished by the new church would equal, and even excel, if possible, that of the time-honored Christian organization of Great St. James Street. 'The present edifice will offer to the eye a much more pleasing aspect than the old walls; but, my dear friends, the good work of saving souls and bettering humanity will call for the same self-sacrifice, the same identical watchfulness and the prayerful solicitude as of old, to ensure the same blessing and glory which attended your labors in the dear old church below. I am glad that this will be a better and more beautiful structure. There is no beauty in ugliness. We cannot look over the beautiful fields, and flowery hillsides, or up into the starry heavens, without being obliged to realize that God looks with pleasure upon fine architecture when dedicated to His work and to His honor and glory. But there is something more important than that which pleases the human eye; it is to feel that the Holy Spirit has found an abiding place within our grand, as well as our most humble, ecclesiastical structures. There is no reason to believe that those noble and devoted men and women who have toiled for the success of Methodism in St. James Street will relax their efforts here, and there is no reason why those who crowded the galleries in the old church may not come here in as great numbers and learn quite as freely both to live and to die. The words so eloquently addressed to you by the last speaker represent the sentiment of all here to-day. There is not the slightest feeling of envy in the hearts of any member of the other Methodist churches when we behold the rapid progress and great power attained by the St. James Street parish. Your good fortune is as much pleasure to us as it is to you. Your success is our success, and I am glad to see among your trustees men who are not members of this particular church, and I rejoice to know that there are rich men of the Dominion Square Church who are freely helping you to bring to an early completion a church which is destined to do so much good for its members and to the community. My wish, which is shared by all my congregation, is that prosperity may attend your labors, and that God's blessing may descend upon all your works.'

ST. JAMES STREET METHODIST CHURCH. 53

"Mr. Philp here rose and introduced the Rev. Mark Guy Pearse, as the representative of the mother country. Mr. Pearse, who was received with loud applause, said he did not know much about the affairs of the Church here, but as the Israelites of old made bricks without straw he would be obliged to make pots without clay. Continuing, the great London orator observed that he was delighted to hear how prosperous the different churches were, and of the amount of God's work which had been done in this city. He said that for many years the name of Senator Ferrier had been a familar one to him, and he greatly rejoiced that at last he was enabled to meet that good man, and wish him many more years of life and happiness, so that he might see this church not only completed but free from all incumbrances.

"The Rev. Dr. Shaw, President of the Conference, on being introduced, said:—' I wish in a few minutes to emphasize three thoughts in connection with this service. 1st. The principle of catholicity upon which this church is to be based. Methodism takes it stand on this magnificent square to-day, not in the attitude of hostility but of honorable rivalry in God's service with other Churches, that we may mutually provoke each other to good works. We believe in denominationalism, but not in sectarianism. By the varied agencies of different denominations the Church has made greater progress during the past one hundred years, than in all the preceding centuries. At the same time, of all Christians we should be most free from sectarian narrowness and strife. Our Church was born in a revival, and not in ecclesiastical and doctrinal controversy. It never formally seceded from any other Church, but appeared to have been unjustly thrust out from the grand old Church from which it sprung; and so we wish to stand here to-day as the friends of all and the enemies of none. We take an advanced position this hour in the brotherhood of Christian churches in this city, with the kindliest feeling to all. The second thought I wished to notice is the variety of equipment which our Church to-day needs in all its appliances, including church buildings. We need large structures, such as the present is designed to be, and others not so ornate; we need the cheap and comfortable mission tabernacle, and we need the log churches in our remote settlements. Methodism has grown so marvellously that it touches society at every point, and what will serve the spiritual interests of one class of people will not suit another. As we gather here to-day in this great commercial metropolis, in this interesting service, we do not forget the brave and noble men who, in shanties and small school-houses and chapels of very unattractive appearance, are this hour toiling amid the hardships and privations of our back missions; men of whom the world is not worthy; men whose names may now be unknown, but who shall be found unto praise, and honor, and glory at the appearing of Jesus Christ. The humbler style of church architecture has its place: but its place, except in the opinion of open foes or doubtful friends, is surely not here, if we would make our church in this city most potent in moving men to God and goodness. In conclusion, I emphasize the fact that this structure, thus initiated has, I believe as its object, the glory of God and the salvation of men. A curse be upon its towers and minarets, its groins and gargoyles, its marbles and frescoes, if these came between Christ and the human soul, and deprived the soul of that definite and experimental consciousness of salvation which is so prominent in the life and history and theology of Methodism. And to this execration, I believe, both pastor and trustees are prepared to say Amen! Let the world know that Methodism is emphatically the Church of the people—not in any loose, destructive sense, but on the contrary, for the uplifting of the people in piety, morality and intelligence, and, therefore, by all will a cordial welcome in this sanctuary be found. This is the first hour of our worship on this square. Let the thought now be emphasized and everywhere enunciated that the church now being here commenced is for the people, to help them to Christ and to heaven; and we have no doubt that, as in the case of its predecessor, it will be the place in which multitudes shall pass from darkness to light. May God grant that it may be so!'

ST. JAMES STREET METHODIST CHURCH. 55

" At the conclusion of Prof. Shaw's address, the Hon. Mr. Ferrier was invited to speak. After recognizing the generous Providence which permitted him to take part in so solemn a demonstration, the speaker said : 'I congratulate you on this event as Methodists, as Christians, and as citizens of the great commercial metropolis of the Dominion. The history of Methodism in this city began with the century. In 1803, the New York Conference appointed the Rev. Nathan Bangs to Montreal. The name ' Dr. Bangs ' is historical in American Methodism. At this early period much kindness was extended to the infant cause by the minister and congregation of the St. Gabriel Presbyterian Church. In 1803, the small church in St. Sulpice Street was opened. That building is still standing, immediately in the rear of Notre Dame Church, as the memorial of the struggles and triumphs of early Methodism. Subsequent to the American war of 1812, the relations of our Church were changed from American to British Methodism. The abounding prosperity of that period led to the erection of a beautiful church at the corner of St. James and St. François Xavier Streets, in 1821. With this church the names of the Rev. Robt. Lusher, the Rev. Dr. Alder, the Rev. William Squire, and the Rev. John Barry—the Apollos of Methodism—are forever associated. Twenty-three years later, in the summer of 1844, it was my privilege and honor to lay the corner-stone of the present St. James Street Church, with which the names of Dr. Richey, the Rev. Charles Churchill, the Rev. Dr. Chas. DeWolfe, and the Rev. Dr. Lachlin Taylor, with many living ministers, are associated. It is believed that there is scarcely a city or town or county, from the Atlantic to the Pacific, from the Mexican Gulf to the Valley of the St. Lawrence, that has not representatives that have worshipped in that time-honored church, while the heavens have received a great cloud of witnesses whose espousals to Christ began within its hallowed walls.'

"Senator Ferrier concluded his address by predicting that the new edifice would be worthy of the old, and a blessing to generations yet unborn.

"The pastor now turned to Mr. Ferrier, and, in feeling tones, presented to him, in the name of the trustees, a very handsome silver trowel, which bore the following inscription: 'Presented to the Hon. Jas. Ferrier by the trustees of St. James Street Church, on the occasion of the laying of the corner-stone of the new Methodist Church on St. Catherine Street, June 11th, 1887.'

"All being ready for the final ceremony—the documents, hermetically sealed in a metal box, were consigned to the cavity prepared for them in the lower section of the massive stone, Mr. A. F. Dunlop, the architect, having personally attended to the laying in of the necessary quantity of cement, the huge upper stone was lowered quietly into its destined position—Senator Ferrier, amidst breathless silence, performed an office which very rarely falls to the lot of man. Forty-three years ago he had laid the corner-stone of the St. James Street Church, and again now he had been called upon to repeat the ceremony. It was on behalf of the same church; but, as the old gentleman spoke with tremulous accents, it was quite evident that he realized how few were left of that former throng which had gathered around him nearly half a century ago. Taking in his hand the small mallet which he had used on the former occasion, and which had been carefully preserved, the father of Montreal Methodism stepped forward and said, striking the stone slowly three times with the mallet: 'I lay this corner-stone in the name of the Father, Son and Holy Ghost. Amen.'

"The Rev. Mr. Philp then invited all present to come and place their offerings upon the stone which had just been so successfully laid. A general response was made to this appeal, and a very handsome sum was collected in a few minutes. 'God save the Queen' was then played by the silver cornet band, which had rendered during the afternoon most excellent service, under the efficient leadership of Mr. G. H. Holland, and the large concourse of people dispersed."

ST. JAMES STREET METHODIST CHURCH.

The following is a copy of the document which was beautifully engrossed by J. H. Elliott, and deposited in the corner-stone:—

In the name of the Father, Son, and Holy Ghost:

The corner-stone of the Methodist Church, erected on St. Catherine Street, in the City of Montreal, for the congregation of the St. James Street Church, was laid,

To the honor and glory of Almighty God, with appropriate ceremonies, by the Hon. James Ferrier, Senator, on the 11th day of June, in the year of our Lord one thousand eight hundred and eighty seven, and in the fiftieth, or Jubilee year of the reign of Her Most Gracious Majesty Queen Victoria.

Trustees: Hon. James Ferrier, James Ferrier, jun., John Torrance, Frederick Fairman, Thomas D. Hood, George Armstrong, George Young, George Douglas, LL.D., Geo. E. Jaques, jun., George Vipond, James McBride, James Griffin, Robert Miller, Dugald Graham, B.C.L., Alfred Ward, Joseph E. Alston, Thos. Nichol, M.D., D.C.L.

Pastor: Rev. John Philp, M.A.

Resident Methodist Ministers of the City of Montreal for the current ecclesiastical year: The Reverends George Douglas, LL.D., William I Shaw, LL.D., William Hansford, John Borland, William Hall, M.A., J. Cooper Antliff, D.D., Stephen Bond, James Henderson, Jabez B. Saunders, M.D., Wm. Jackson, Alexander Campbell, and Ernest Manley Taylor.

President of Montreal Conference: Rev. William I. Shaw, LL.D.

General Superintendents of the Methodist Church: Rev. A Carman, D.D., Rev. J. A. Williams, D.D.

Governor-General: Henry Charles Keith Petty Fitzmaurice Marquis of Lansdowne.

Ex-Pastors of this Church, from 1803 to 1846 : Samuel Merwin, Martin Ruter, S. Coates, Nathan Bangs, T. Madden, J. Scull, J. Mitchell, Thomas Burch, Richard Williams, J. B. Strong, John DePutron, W. Brown, James Booth, W. Bardow, Richard Pope, Robert L. Lusher, E. Bowen, A. Sieger, John Hick, T. Dixon, James Knowlan, Henry Pope, Robert Alder, Joseph Stinson, William Squire, William Croscombe, John Barry, William Lord, Matthew Richey, W. M. Harvard, John B. Selley, M.D., Edmund Botterell, Richard Hutchinson, John P. Hetherington, John Borland, Robert Cooney, Charles Churchill, A.M., George H. Davis.

From 1847 to 1887 : Matthew Richey, D.D., Chas. Churchill, A.M., John Jenkins, D.D., Charles DeWolfe, Lachlan Taylor, William Squire, G. N. A. F. T. Dickson, George Douglas, LL.D., Jas. H. Bishop, Wellington Jeffers, D.D., John Gemley, Isaac B. Howard, Ephraim B. Harper, D.D., James Elliott, D.D., Chas. Lavell, M.A., William Briggs, D.D., John B. Clarkson, M.A., John Potts, D.D., Alexander Sutherland, D.D., Leonard Gaetz, Benjamin Longley, M.A., Hugh Johnston, M.A., D. E. Mallory. John Potts, D.D., John Philp, M.A.

Synopsis on the History of Methodism in Montreal :

1802—Montreal visited by the Rev. Joseph Sawyer, of New York Conference of the Methodist Episcopal Church, U. S. First class formed.

1803—First Methodist Minister stationed in Montreal—Rev. S. Merwin, of the New York Conference.

1808—First Methodist Church built on St. Sulpice Street, (then St. Joseph Street) still standing (1887), in rear of Notre Dame Church.

1815—First Wesleyan Methodist Minister, from England, stationed in Montreal.

1819—First Methodist Missionary Auxiliary formed in Canada. On account of the church on St. Sulpice Street being too small, the meeting was held in the St. Gabriel Street Presbyterian Church, which was kindly loaned for the purpose.

ST. JAMES STREET METHODIST CHURCH. 59

1820—Withdrawal of the American Methodist missionaries in harmony with agreement made between the Wesleyan Methodist Church of England and the Methodist Episcopal Church of the United States.

1821—St. Sulpice Church superseded by a new and larger one on the corner of St. James and St. François Xavier Streets, the lot now occupied by the Medical Hall.

1827—Chapel in Gain Street, Quebec suburbs, built—a class having been organized in that locality by Mr. John Mathewson the previous year.

1834—Jan. 21. Wellington Street Church (near McGill Street) opened; sermons preached at dedicatory service by the Rev. Messrs. Croscombe, Squire and Barry.

1837—The Gain Street congregation removed to the St. Mary Street Chapel, a building which was fitted up for public services by the Hon. James Ferrier.

1845—The present Lagauchetiere Street Church opened under the superintendency of the Rev. M. Richey, A.M., and occupied by the congregation from St. Mary Street.

1845—May 27. The present St. James Street Church opened, with sermons by Rev. Messrs. Richey, Carruthers (Congregational), and Churchill, and with large congregations, including His Excellency Lord Metcalfe (Governor-General) and suite. Hon. Jas. Ferrier, Chairman of the Building Committee.

1847—Jan. 20. The Wellington Street Church having been burnt, the late Ottawa Street Church was opened.

1854—Union of the Lower Canada District, which had hitherto been under the direct supervision of the British Conference, with the Wesleyan Methodist Church of Canada.

1856—Salem New Connexion Methodist Church in Panet Street opened.

1857—Ebenezer New Connexion Methodist Church, in Dupre Lane, opened.

1865—Dominion Square, Sherbrooke Street, and Point St.

Charles Churches opened, as the result of a church extension scheme organized in 1864.

1869—West End Church opened.

1873—Wesleyan Theological College founded.

1874—Union of the Wesleyan Methodist Church of Canada, the New Connexion Methodist Church, and the Wesleyan Methodist Church of Eastern British America, together to be called the Methodist Church of Canada.

1875—Douglas Church opened.

1878—First French Methodist Church, Craig Street, opened.

1883—Union of the Methodist Church of Canada, the Methodist Episcopal Church of Canada, the Primitive Methodist and Bible Christian Churches of Canada, together to be called the Methodist Church.

1886—Lecture room of the Mountain Street Church opened.

1887—June 11. In the Jubilee year of the reign of Her Most Gracious Majesty Queen Victoria, the corner-stone of the new church on St. Catherine Street laid by the Hon. Senator Ferrier.

The above historical synopsis was prepared by the Rev. Dr. Shaw from files of journals, histories, official records and conversations with aged members of the Church, among others the Hon. James Ferrier, the late John Mathewson and Wm. Lunn.

In this bottle are deposited the following coins:—Canadian fifty cents, twenty-five cents, ten cents and five cents silver pieces; a Canadian bronze one cent piece. Also copies of the following newspapers and periodicals:—*Christian Guardian*, of Toronto; *Christian Advocate*, of Montreal; *Montreal Daily Witness*, *Montreal Daily Star*, and *Montreal Gazette*, Report of Missionary Society of the Methodist Church. Publications of Methodist Book-Room, Toronto:—*Methodist Magazine*, *The Sunbeam*, *Happy Days*, *Home and School*, *Pleasant Hours*.

Rev. W. I. Shaw, LL.D.,
Rev. John Borland,   } Committee.
G. E. Jaques, Jun.,

A Glimpse at St. James'—Old and New.

(From the " Bazaar Souvenir.")

Few churches in Canada, if indeed any, can boast of a grander record than the church which forms the subject of the present sketch. If it cannot lay claim to rival in antiquarian interest some other structures in our land, at least, it has no cause to be ashamed of its career. If the successive edifices erected during the progress of its history do not call forth the ardent admiration of the friends of art, it can glory in a record of a nobler kind, and vastly more enduring character.

First Methodist Church, 1807.

Cradled in this place, Canadian Methodism went forth to spread its teachings far and wide, and the present building yet remains the centre of an interest and influence felt over all this vast Dominion; and far away over the dark waters of the peaceful ocean the shadow of this influence makes itself felt in Japan.

Could these walls but speak, how their tale would thrill the heart of every loyal Methodist; how their message would recall to the mind of many an aged member the hallowed scenes of long ago, awakening fresh memories of faces once beloved, now passed away'; once eager to fulfil their share of duty, now gone to reap reward of service! How there would echo round us the memory of many a voice once all on fire with living, burning eloquence, proclaiming the Gospel from its pulpit, or leading the sweet songs of Zion from its choir; or, in the more social service, giving their testimony, ringing, sharp and clear.

Here multitudes of Christians had their birth; this church has been a nursery of souls, and a school for developing Christian character for well-nigh four score years, and who shall essay to count the number of those who, blessed by its teachings and its prayers, and thus first prepared, have left it to join the host triumphant round the throne. Verily, here has been situated a gate of heaven. This church is in very deed the Westminster Abbey of Canadian Methodism, the City Road of Canada.

A glance, brief and hurried it must be, at a few of the leading events—a glimpse at a few of the more familiar faces of the past—would not, we think, come amiss at the present juncture, when the congregation are about to emigrate from the scenes of such triumphs, to set up the standard on higher ground. According to Moister, the mission historian, Methodism was introduced into Canada by one Tuffy, a soldier in the army of King George, who held the first Methodist service with his fellow soldiers in the city of Quebec, in 1780. The first Methodist Society was formed in Upper Canada in 1791, by William Losee, where a few years before it had been introduced by a zealous Irish local preacher, George Neal.

Methodism is first heard of in Montreal in the year 1803, when Joseph Sawyer paid a passing visit and organized the first class-meeting. The following year, 1804, Samuel Merwin was appointed the first resident minister, the membership at the time being only nineteen. During the next four or five years the Methodists of the city were without a regular preaching place; but in the year 1807, it was decided to erect a building to be specially set apart for the worship of God. A site on St. Joseph Street (now St. Sulpice Street) was selected, and the first Methodist church was erected, and opened in the year 1808. This building still stands, having been sold for a news-room in 1821, and subsequently transferred to the authorities of the Notre Dame Church.

During the troublous times of 1812-14 Methodism firmly held its ground, but the war of those years plainly left its influence on the people, and it was deemed wise to recall some of the American ministers, who, up to that time, had been the sole occupants of the field, and to supply their places with mission-

SECOND METHODIST CHURCH, 1821.

aries from England. Hence it was that in 1814, Richard Williams and Joseph B. Strong came out from the Old Country, and became the first Wesleyan missionaries to settle in Montreal. In the year 1820, the American ministers finally withdrew.

Montreal Methodists have always felt the importance of missions; therefore the year 1819 should be dear to all lovers of missions, as the date of the first missionary meeting held in "St. James'." On this occasion the trustees of the St. Gabriel Church generously lent their building, as the Methodist chapel was thought to be too small; and this fact, more than any other, led to the erection of a more spacious edifice, in the year 1821, on the corner of St. James and St. François Xavier Streets. This church, Bosworth, in his "Hochelaga Depicta," thus describes: "It is a cut stone building, the architecture is of the Grecian Doric order, with a portico corresponding. It is galleried all round, and has a fine organ. It is justly considered as one of the most beautiful edifices of its kind in the city." The cost of erection amounted to £6,000. In this building for the following twenty-five years Montreal Methodism had its home; there quietly, yet none the less powerfully, did it make its influence felt, drawing many to its communion and fellowship. So rapid, indeed, was its growth, that the membership which, at its opening, numbered 119, had increased in the year 1845 to 770.

Like its predecessor, the church of 1821 began to be felt too small for the congregation, and the present building, known as Great St. James Street Church, was resolved on in 1844.

The ceremony of laying the corner-stone of this church was a gala scene for its friends. The most notable features of the day were, a grand procession of officers and members, marshalled by John Sproston and James L. Mathewson, marching from the old church to the new, and laying the corner-stone by James Ferrier, Esq., who, 42 years after, as Senator Ferrier, had the singular honor of performing a similar ceremony for the fourth church, the mallet used being the same on both occasions.

The church was opened for public worship, July 27th, 1845, when Rev. Dr. Richey, the Bradburn of Canadian Methodism, preached the dedicatory sermon, and Governor-General Lord Metcalfe attended in state, and materially aided the trustees in their efforts.

It is still the largest Methodist church in the city; its dimensions are 111x73 feet. The cost of erection was £13,000. The pulpit is justly regarded the finest of its kind in Canada.

In this temple Methodism has had its centre for 42 years. From it, during that time, many of its members have gone forth, and, aided by the generosity of its trustees, have erected other Methodist churches throughout the city, the sum devoted to this purpose reaching the splendid total of $80,000. The congregation has done its full share of philanthropic and mission work. As is well known, most of the large annual meetings of the great Protestant Societies have been held within its walls, and each New Year's Day there has been gathered together all the

THIRD METHODIST CHURCH, 1845.

Methodist Sunday-school scholars of the city; their appearance and singing forming a sight never to be forgotten by those who have had the privilege to enjoy one.

But, during all these years, Montreal, as a city, has been rapidly growing and spreading. Many streets which, forty years ago, were considered as being in the best residential part of the town, are now devoted exclusively to commercial purposes. On this account, there has been for some years past a conviction that it would be desirable to secure a site and build a church up town; and, despite the great reluctance felt at leaving a home hallowed by so many associations, the conviction took tangible form last year, when an addition was made to the Trust Board of the Centre Circuit, and the Allan property secured for building purposes for the sum of $70,000. Steps were at once taken to have plans prepared for the proposed new building. In order to secure as much information as possible, the trustees commissioned their pastor and secretary to visit the principal churches in New York and Chicago in order to get as many hints as possible, and the result, we hope, will give us a church beautiful on the exterior, and in the interior fitted up with every modern convenience.

The dimensions are as follows:—

```
Length from south to north ..................... 253 feet
Width of Transepts ............................. 106  "
Height of Great Tower .......................... 200  "
Height of Lesser Tower ......................... 140  "
Height of Church proper, from ground to apex of roof.. 92  "
```
Seating accommodation provided for 2,500 people.
The school-room will hold 1,000 persons.

The church, when completed, will, without doubt, form one of the grandest ornaments of the city, and will gain the character of being the finest Protestant ecclesiastical edifice in Canada. The class-rooms, parlors, instrument and appliances will be all of the most modern and approved character.

Of the men who have stood at the helm, and guided the affairs of the Church for close on a century, our space permits of only the barest notice.

Amongst its ministers have been some of the most distinguished men in Methodism. Here, in the past, have been stationed Alder and Stinson, Harvard and Richey, Jenkins and Jeffers. In more recent years the congregation has been benefited and blessed by the ministrations of Revs. Drs. Douglas, Potts, Sutherland, Leonard Gaetz, Hugh Johnston and others.

ST. JAMES STREET METHODIST CHURCH. 67

Almost every distinguished English minister who has been in this country has occupied its pulpit—Dixon and Thornton, Wiseman, Dallinger and Coley, Arthur and Smith and Jobson, Joseph Parker and Newman Hall, Caughey, the Revivalist, and, most renowed of all, William Morley Punshon, the Apollos of Methodism and the anointed king of modern pulpit eloquence. The United States, too, has sent many of her most distinguished sons

FOURTH METHODIST CHURCH, 1888.

to greet us—William Taylor, the prince of missionaries; Butler, the Evangelist of India and Mexico; Tiffany, Bishop James, Newman, Peck, Beecher, and many others, have been here, and left behind the fragrance of an eloquence that will not soon be forgotten.

The roll of St. James' honored laymen is very long. Daniel Fisher appears to stand out the most prominently in connection with the first church. The names of John and David Torrance, of John and Samuel Mathewson, of Thomas Kay and William Lunn, of Robert Campbell, and Richard Latham and John Hilton will be inseparably associated with the memory of the second church.

While standing out from all others in bold relief is the honored name, James Ferrier; connected with first church on St. James Street, mainly influential in the erection of the present church, lending to all schemes of the Church a wonderful energy of character, and an almost faultless soundness of judgment. The most princely supporter of Methodism in Canada, Senator Ferrier yet survives, at the advanced age of nearly ninety years, to give the new building project his strong support and sympathy. It is the prayerful wish of all that his life may yet long be spared, and that he will be able to preside at the opening ceremonies next October. Of the men who are now bearing the burden and heat of the day in connection with the progressing erection, it is needless to make mention. Of them it may be said, as of a certain leading architect of old, "If you seek their monument, look around."

With every advantage of position and site, with the largest Protestant congregation in the city, with tenfold better accommodation and appliances, it is the prayer of the many members and friends of this undertaking that the new church shall go forth to prove herself the superior of her three older sisters, not alone in the things of mere material character and temporal interest, but that, in the loftier and grander sphere of the spiritual and eternal, she shall develop the high ideal of the primitive Church; that pentecostal power shall constantly attend the preaching of her pastors, and the prayers of her people, and that she shall still be considered worthy, as of yore, to be called a centre of religious influence and stronghold of Heaven until, in the progress of the years, the time shall come for her to make way for her successor.

ST. JAMES STREET METHODIST CHURCH.

"The Lord loveth the gates of Zion, more than all the dwellings of Jacob."—*David.*

"But will God indeed dwell on the earth."—*Solomon.*

"Behold the tabernacle of God is with men, and He will dwell with them."—*St. John.*

What tender memories throng around the dear old Church of St. James! Not half a century has elapsed since our venerable Senator laid the foundation-stone, and yet, not a few lives have been rounded there. Baptismal, bridal and burial services. Buds, blossoms and withered leaves. The wondering eye and inarticulate lisp of infancy; the blushing cheek and faltering "I will" of maidenhood; the marble brow and quiet bosom within the "narrow house."

St. James Church has been indeed a Bethel—has been a Bethlehem—the house of the "All-father," wherein the bread of life has been broken to His hungry children. Where the wanderer has often found a home; the dark mind been enlightened, the ignorant instructed, the drooping cheered, the mourner comforted, the weak made strong, and the dead in sin raised to life and light.

It has been a "fortress," to which the righteous have resorted for safety; a "pavilion," wherein they have been hidden from the strife of tongues; "the shadow of a great rock in a weary land;" a "banqueting house," wherein God's banner over His people has been "Love."

Still brighter hopes cluster around and illumine our rising sanctuary. We go from the old to the new, in the faith that it is from good to better—to multiplying "Trinities of benediction." We shall inscribe "Peace" upon its open portals, and "Welcome" within its walls. It shall be, as the seraphic poet puts it, "A cloud and a smoke by day, the shining of a flaming fire by night; for upon all the glory shall be a defence; a place of refuge, and a covert from storm, and from rain."

It shall be a storehouse, with vaster supplies of heavenly manna, where ever-increasing multitudes shall be supplied with bread.

" Green pastures " and " still waters," where the droppings of the showers shall swell to torrents and to floods. Where the rays of promise that hitherto have smiled upon us, shall broaden into the noonday splendor of the " Sun of Righteousness."

A " house of prayer," where the soul's softest whisper shall ever find the open ear of God ; a " holy place," where man shall be " new made"; a portico of heaven, where the melody of glad human voices shall rise and mingle with the deathless songs of the redeemed.

Financial History of the Church.

We would now take a short review of the financial history of the church.

Of the cost, and list of subscribers, of the first church in 1808, we have no record, further than the fact that the most of the money was raised in England.

The cost of the church of 1820 was, for the ground, £1,350, and for the building, £3,200 ; total, £4,550, or $18,200.

This was made up as follows :—

Proceeds sale of old church	£1,000	0	0
Collected in Quebec	52	15	1
Collected in Montreal from 109 contributors	1,134	2	6
Collection at opening of church	42	12	6
Loaned by R. McGinnis for 8 years without interest, and then at 6 per cent.	500	0	0
Loaned from others	1,820	9	11
Total	£4,550	0	0

Of the 108 contributors, the largest was £300 ($1,500), from Mrs. Margaret Hutchinson, afterwards Mrs. Lunn ; and the smallest (5s. 6d.), $1.10, is credited to "a poor woman"; the remainder varied from 10s. to £201 5s. Daniel Fisher's name is credited with £201 5s., and the firm of D. & J. Fisher, with £75.

We would commend to our friends the example of Mr. R. McGinnis, who gave a straight subscription of £50, and then an additional £3, and *lent without interest for eight years* a sum of £500. This, for the time being, assisted the funds of the new church as materially as if it had been given outright, and after the lapse of that time the church was quite able then to meet the charge of interest, from the greater revenue coming in from the enlarged congregation and membership which the increased facilities of the new church had provided.

The cost of the present St. James' was as follows:—

For expenses of meetings, March, 1844, to consider the question of building three new churches— Rev. Mr. Lusher's expenses, $12; Rev. Mr. Squire's, $30; Rev. Mr. Richey's, $40	$82 00
Cost of circulars calling the meetings	7 00
G. L. Dickinson, architect, premium for best plan	40 00
Cost of land	18,206 50
Cost of building, including first organ	37,627 53
Cost of font	184 65
Total	$56,147 68

Towards this sum the trustees received:—

Sale of old church	$17,395 25
Collection on plate at opening of church	436 57
Subscription at opening of church	32,058 28
Total	$49,890 10

It is evident that, had one church only been built at that time, the financing would have been an easy matter. But the Lagauchetiere Street Church (East End) was built about the same time by the St. James Street Church Trustees, and in 1847 the Ottawa Street Church was also built by them. The revenue from these two churches was but small, and the burden of sustentation of the three causes fell on the Centre. That this was no light matter will be evident from a glimpse at the abstract statement of receipts and expenditures of the trustees from the opening of the church to the present date, as exhibited on page 93. From this it will be seen that the cost of East End Church, including expenses from opening until handed over to a new Trustee Board, and deducting therefrom all receipts from said church left at the

ST. JAMES STREET METHODIST CHURCH.

debit of the St. James Board, was $23,401.39, and for the Ottawa Street Church, until taken over by a Board of their own members, the cost was $27,703.91. From 1846 until 1855 nothing material was done towards reducing the debts thus incurred, and the charge for interest was increasing and becoming very oppressive, and it was not an uncommon thing for the trustees to have to divide up among themselves the annual deficiency, and each pay his own share of the same.

The trustees decided, in 1855, to appeal to the people for help in the matter. The troubles caused by the then recent division of the circuit had seriously impaired the revenues from the East End and Ottawa Street Churches, and the financial position was very embarrassing. A clear, plain statement of the finances was for the first time laid before a public meeting of the whole congregation, and the result was a subscription list that yielded $51,374.88. Thus has it ever been among Methodists. When there has been a plain statement shown that money is wanted, that it is really needed, and some good assurance that it will be well and judiciously expended, it will always be subscribed. The payments of the subscriptions upon this occasion were spread over a period of six years, and after they were paid the debt on the church ceased to be a burden.

The people of the three churches having thus for six years, in addition to meeting the working expenses of their own churches, been paying these extra amounts, ranging, according to the ability of the subscriber, from one dollar a year to one hundred dollars a year, and as none of them had in any way suffered from these extra payments, a want seemed to be felt among them for some desirable worthy object towards which they might still continue their payments. And the general Church Extension movement was organized, the outcome of which was the building of Dominion Square, Sherbrooke Street, Point St. Charles and West End Churches. A meeting was held in St. James Street Church to talk the matter over, and over $34,000 was subscribed at once, and the meeting was adjourned until the following Wednesday, as a large number of people known to be favorable to the cause were unavoidably absent. At this second meeting the amount was increased to nearly $60,000. To show the spirit in which this matter was taken up, one young man, earning $500 per annum, attended the first meeting, and put down his name for $50. On going home, he mentioned to his mother what had been done at the meeting, and told her that he had subscribed $50. "Oh," she replied, "that is not like a Methodist subscription; you can very well afford more." He thought the matter over, and came to the conclusion that he could afford more, and went to the adjourned meeting and sent up his card for $100, in place of $50 promised last week.

The arrangement for the division of the Church Extension Fund was that of all the money thus raised—Sixth-twelfths were to go to the Dominion Square Trustees; four-twelfths to the Sherbrooke Street Trustees; one-twelfth to the Point St. Charles Trustees; one-twelfth to the West End Trustees. The Trustees of St. James Street Church made a grant of $6,300 towards this fund.

On the opening of the West End Church in 1869, when the debt was found to be so large, and beyond the ability of their own congregation to take care of, the Centre Trustees undertook to meet the interest on $4,000 at 7 per cent. for five years; amounting in all to $1,400, and at the conclusion of the five years made them an additional grant of $1,000.

In addition to all these sums the Trustees presented the Wesleyan Theological College with a sum of $10,000, payable at their convenience, but subject to interest until paid. It will thus be seen that every Methodist church in Montreal, as well as the college, has been directly helped from the funds of St. James', with the single exception of the Douglas Church.

The amounts thus given will figure up as follows:

East End		$23,401 39
Ottawa Street		27,703 91
Church Extension Fund:		
Six-twelfths, Dominion Square	$3,150 00	
Four-twelfths, Sherbrooke Street	2,100 00	
One-twelfth, Point St. Charles	525 00	
One-twelfth, West End	525 00	
		6,300 00
West End, interest on $4,000, five years		1,400 00
West End, special grant		1,000 00
Wesleyan Theological College	$10,000 00	
Do. do. Interest until paid	8,811 30	
		18,811 30
		$78,616 60

There were apparently two courses open to the trustees in 1846: to build and work for themselves only, or to work for Methodism generally in the city. Had they chosen the first course, it would have been very easy to finance. As shown on page 72, the cost of the Centre Church was $56,147.68 and the available assets $49,890.10—a deficiency of only $6,257.58. The rents from the two stores adjoining the church could have met the interest on that small amount of debt.

It may, perhaps, be possible that some part of the subscriptions raised at that time, $32,058, may have been given only on account of the great work of building three churches all at once. But if even one-half had been withheld, the burden remaining would have been very small. However, after a lapse of over forty years, the general verdict will no doubt be one of general commendation of the energy and zeal shown by the original nine trustees.

The heavy liabilities incurred at the time made it absolutely necessary that the people should give above the average, or they would have sunk under the weight they were carrying. When the immediate necessity for these extra gifts ceased, the habits of liberal giving had been formed, and the givers looked around for other objects towards which to bestow their liberality; hence, as one fund had been provided for, another was taken up. This has been, next to the children's giving, the real secret of the large Missionary gifts which have made Montreal rank so far ahead of any other city. Other cities may have given, at times, more in the aggregate than Montreal has done, but when comparisons have been made of man for man, no one has yet approached her within 60 cents to the dollar; and as to our Sunday-schools, as shown in a letter to the *Christian Guardian*, in March, 1886, the Missionary givings of 1,000 children, from all parts of Ontario, did not even equal what was sent in from twenty-six of our own scholars. Many of us, who were ourselves children in the schools collecting for the Missionary Society, have been gratified to see our children engaged in the same blessed work, and sending in amounts that make our collections of former days pale into insignificance. We trust that it may ever be the chief characteristic of Montreal Methodism, that they honor the Lord with the first-fruits of all their increase.

We have some amongst us who are looking forward with great apprehension to the greatly increased working expenses which we shall have to provide for in our new church, and to see exactly how we stand, we ask attention to the statement appended, showing receipts and expenditure for twenty years past. In this statement all revenue from rents is excluded, as there will be none when the stores are sold : and we also leave out of the expenditure all grants, taking up the working expenses only of the church, and leaving the interest to be discussed separately.

From this exhibit it will be seen that for five years from 1868-72, there was a surplus of $6,550.76 of receipts over expenditure; the succeeding five years the surplus was $4,819.92. From 1878-82 the receipts were down considerably, and the surplus was only $216.78 for the five years, but they make a better appearance in the last term, netting $3,618.87 over the expenditure.

ST. JAMES STREET METHODIST CHURCH.

Receipts from Plate Collections and Pew Rents.

YEAR.	PLATE COL.	PEW R'NTS.	TOTAL.	EXPENSES.	SURPLUS.
1868	$1190 92	$2571 65	$3762 57	$1952 19	
1869	1135 34	2377 41	3512 75	3088 01	
1870	1205 04	2963 91	4168 95	2889 01	
1871	1404 73	2483 38	3888 11	2335 20	
1872	1528 99	2560 35	4089 34	2606 55	
	$6465 02	$12956 70	$19421 72	$12890 96	$6550 76
1873	1547 63	2778 63	4326 26	2747 27	
1874	1473 33	3803 99	5277 32	3568 39	
1875	1663 43	3495 97	5159 40	5777 28	
1876	1666 99	3112 99	4779 98	2615 51	
1877	1543 18	2541 74	4084 92	4099 51	
	$7894 56	$15733 32	$23627 88	$18807 96	4819 92
1878	1261 65	2237 89	3499 54	3730 19	
1879	1252 78	2437 83	3690 61	5323 39	
1880	1179 66	2061 74	3241 40	2380 28	
1881	886 92	2002 35	2889 27	2767 77	
1882	1052 10	2379 07	3431 17	2333 58	
	$5633 11	$11118 88	$16751 99	$16535 21	216 78
1883	1430 19	1967 78	3397 97	2459 69	
1884	1388 48	2435 27	3823 75	3306 58	
1885	1522 82	2249 88	3792 70	3454 92	
1886	1528 83	2308 25	3837 08	2819 60	
1887	1322 20	2347 85	3670 05	2841 89	
	$7192 52	$11309 03	$18501 55	$14882 68	3618 87

There are some features in connection with our work of building churches in the past that are encouraging to meditate on at the present. There are those who deprecated the expenditure of so much money for land for our new church enterprise, looking for dire consequences from such, as they think, uncalled-for prodigality. We would ask such to consider the relative amounts paid for the two churches built on St. James Street. In 1820, the trustees sold their old church, land and building and all, for four thousand dollars ($4,000), and paid five thousand four hundred dollars ($5,400) for land only on which to put up their building, putting their hands in their pockets and their signatures on paper to meet *the whole cost of their building and the balance due on land.*

In 1845, the church of 1820, land and building, was sold for $17,395.25, and the amount paid for the land only for the present site was $18,206.50 ; and, as on the former occasion, *the whole cost of the new buildings had to be provided for by subscriptions.*

Now, as we expect to get over two hundred thousand for our present site, had we acted on the precedent of the two former occasions, we would have given in excess of this sum for land only ; and as the amount paid for land was $70,000, we start on the comparative basis $130,000 to the good.

For the church of 1820 the largest number of subscribers gave £5, or $20 each. In 1846 the liberality of the people had increased as well as their means, as we find the subscriptions on that occasion to have averaged $100, while twelve years later, for the Church Relief Fund they were able and willing to average £10 a year for six years, or $240. Thus we see a decided advance each time the church is enlarged, and we look for a corresponding increase for our present movement, and we shall not be disappointed. The aggregate amount given by the Board of Trustees of 1846 amounted to $5,100, while our present Board have already given $19,000.

We have, so far, said a good deal about what has been done in the past. But we want to live in the present. A retrospect is

ST. JAMES STREET METHODIST CHURCH. 79

useful to encourage us for the future. Our prospects are encouraging, but the work before us is great, and we must boldly face it.

Our new church, when opened, will have a considerable debt on it, and the duty of the hour will be for us to wipe off that debt as quickly as possible. This is not the church of the trustees, nor the church of the class-leaders, but the church of the people; and what is wanted is that every individual now attending our present St. James Street Church should realize a personal interest in the new edifice, and there is no way in which this can be so well done as by every man, woman and child owning at least one brick, or, if they would like it better, paying for one foot of the ground. The cost of the land having been about one dollar a square foot, they may consider they are paying for as many feet as they give dollars.

Will it be with us as with the children of Israel at the building of the tabernacle? as recorded in Exodus xxxvi. 5-7 : "And they spake unto Moses, saying, The people bring much more than enough for the service of the work which the Lord commanded to make. And Moses gave commandment, and they caused it to be proclaimed throughout the camp, saying, Let neither man nor woman make any more work for the offering of the sanctuary. So the people were restrained from bringing. For the stuff they had was sufficient for all the work to make it, and too much."

It would not be too much to ask, and at the same time be a practical way of giving material aid, if at the opening services every individual attending our church should put upon the plate not less than the full earnings of two days of the previous week. We have a large number of young men and young women who are earning from two dollars to ten dollars a week, they will not find it hard to calculate the proportion for two days. There are many young men in offices earning from $100 to $1,000 a year, it will be easy for them to figure up the exact amount they earn in two days ; and we have also among us business men earning from $1,000 to $10,000 per annum, as well as those whose money-making days are over, and who are quietly living on the honest accumulations of the days that have gone. With all of these, it will not be too much to ask for just two days' income. Of course, no one will be hindered from giving three days' pay, should he so desire, unless the amount thus paid in should be so large as to render necessary a command such as Moses gave, and the people require to be restrained.

We hope that we have not among us any people, so eloquently described at a recent anniversary meeting, who are always on hand at any popular meeting, listening attentively and applauding vehemently, but when a meeting is announced for securing subscriptions for a new building, are found absent—all ears, but no hands—but then, after the building is erected, to which they have contributed not a cent, when any friend from a distance is in their company, will be sure to press them to come and see their beautiful building, of which they are so proud.

Missionary Contributions.

The amounts raised for missionary purposes by the Montreal Methodist Sunday-schools has always been very large. The first date of which we have accurate returns is 1851, when the amount returned by St. James Street Schools was $83.26, and the total from the schools of the city of Montreal, $236.93. We have not had access to the minute books prior to this date. From 1851 to 1887, both inclusive, the total raised by the children of Montreal First Circuit has been $29,046.27, and the total from all the Montreal Methodist Schools, $72,504.38.

The annual gathering of the children on New Year's morning, and the teachers' tea-meeting during the same week, has no doubt largely contributed to this result, giving fresh inspiration for the work of the ensuing year.

The teaching of the Montreal Schools has tended to develop in the minds of the young an interest in missions, and also has educated them to give their own money, thus teaching them self-denial, and also has taught them how to collect. The home boxes have been the receptacle of many a cent that would otherwise have been used to purchase candy, while the collecting cards have developed what powers might be latent of collecting from others. Both means have their uses. Many instances might be given of self-denial encouraged. We will mention a few cases. A young lad asked his father, in case he did without sugar in his tea, would his father give him the cost of the sugar that would be saved, and he would put it in the missionary box. This was agreed to, and the value of the sugar placed at ten cents a month. A younger brother, who heard the bargain made, said he would do the same; but, said he, I will do without sugar in my porridge, which is worth five cents more. So these two boys, under ten years of age, practised self-denial, and gave between them twenty-five cents per month towards our great Missionary enterprises. As the average amount contributed by our whole Church throughout the Dominion is about one dollar per year for each member, it will be seen that these two lads gave as much as three adults.

Another instance: A little girl of eight years of age, who lived some distance from her school, was allowed five cents a day to come home in the street car. Whenever the weather was favorable, she walked home, and put the five cents in her missionary-box.

Self-denial thus encouraged and developed becomes habit, and when the children become men and women their early love for the Missionary Society does not forsake them. As an instance, a year or two ago, two gentlemen, who had been connected with our schools from their early years, met in a train coming into Montreal and got talking about Missionary subscriptions, and one said to the other that he was surprised to see from the Missionary reports that the Recording Steward of the Methodist Church of the town they had just left had only given $2 to the Missionary Society, while they knew he was worth as much as either of them. These two Montrealers were in the habit of giving, with their families, about fifty dollars a year each. The difference in the two city people giving $50 each, and the other only $2, altogether arose from the early training of the Montreal schools, in self-denial and thought for the cause of God.

The total contributed from St. James Street Church to the Missionary Society from 1856, the date of union with Upper Canada Conference, until 1887 amounted to $111,328.90.

It will be remembered that, in 1855, a great effort was made to reduce the debt, and subscriptions were taken, with payments extending over six years, the last of which thus fell due in 1861. It was the year succeeding (the debt being now provided for) that attention was turned to the Missionary Society, and the givings from that date became considerably increased. In 1861, the amount was $1,041.88; in 1862, $2,892.02; and in 1863, $5,280.90. The largest amount ever given was in 1875, when the handsome sum of $6,160.71 was reached.

We publish in full the report of the first year that Montreal appeared in the Canada Conference, both as it calls to mind the active workers of thirty years ago—but few of whom are with us to-day—and also because it shows how the practice of liberality tends to enlarge our conception of the obligation to give on a scale worthy of the cause. These subscriptions were thought large when given, but would be to-day considered small, in the light of what has subsequently been given by the same parties.

We also append the first mention of the Montreal circuits in the reports of the Missionary Society of the Canada Conference in 1856. The list of the missions of that day is interesting.

The first mention of the Montreal circuits in connection with the Missionary Society of the Canada Conference is in 1856, and reads as follows :—

The final local arrangements for the transfer of the missions in Eastern Canada not being entirely terminated at the publication of the committee's last annual report, the following missions then were not included in the Society's printed stations, as they now are for the year 1856–57. Nor are they, for that reason, included in the introductory statistics of this report; but early in the year the transfer took place, and appropriations were made adapted to the peculiar and urgent, because Popish, circumstances of the missionaries; consequently the Society has sustained from its funds this year these missions, besides those regularly reported, and now publishes the Missionary contributions secured from Eastern Canada. It is with great pleasure the committee insert the interesting communications from the esteemed Eastern missionaries, as they rejoice to know that the transfer so cordially made by the parent Conference in Great Britain is already resulting well, spiritually and financially, by the blessing of Divine Providence.

Then follow reports from Rawdon, Wesleyville, Saint John's, Odelltown, Russeltown, Point Levis, Three Rivers, Leeds, Chaudiere, Melbourne, Sherbrooke, Eaton, Dudswell, East Bolton, Shefford, St. Armand and Clarenceville.

First Missionary Report from Montreal Centre Circuit, 1855-1856.

	£	s	d		£	s	d
John Torrance	10	0	0	John Sproston	0	10	0
David Torrance	12	10	0	Rev. W. Jeffers	1	5	0
Hon. James Ferrier	12	10	0	Mr. Hutchinson	1	5	0
John Henderson	6	18	6	Dr. D. C. McCallum	1	5	0
James Ferrier, jun.	10	0	0	Mr. Teesley	1	5	0
Robert Campbell	10	0	0	Mrs. Kay	1	0	0
James A. Mathewson	5	0	0	" Ferrier	1	0	0
George D. Ferrier	5	0	0	" Hall	0	10	0
James H. Henderson	5	0	0	" R. Campbell	0	10	0
Thomas Kay	3	15	0	" White	0	6	3
John Barry	2	10	0	" Jeffrey	0	5	0
George Robson	2	10	0	" Latham	0	5	0
John Hilton	2	10	0	" Baird	0	5	0
Foley & Elliott	2	10	0	" R. Smith	0	5	0
Wm. Lunn	2	10	0	" Cunningham	0	5	0
John Sinclair	2	10	0	" G. D. Ferrier	0	7	6
Richard Latham	2	10	0	George Armstrong	0	5	0
Dr. G. W. Campbell	2	16	0	Mrs. Brandon	0	5	0
W. F. Kay	1	5	0	Mrs. Benn	0	5	0
T. M. Bryson	1	5	0	Mr. & Mrs. Brown	10	0	0
R. & A. Miller	1	5	0	Mrs. G. W. Campbell	2	10	0
S. Gerrard	1	5	0	" A. T. Galt	2	10	0
Wm. Stephens	2	10	0	" John Torrance	1	5	0
R. Carse	1	5	0	" Vanneck	1	5	0
J. & M. Nichols	1	5	0	" D. Torrance	1	0	0
Alex. Empey	1	5	0	Miss E. Jaques' Miss. Box	0	15	0
James Foster	2	10	0	" E. Torrance's "	0	10	2
Wm. Hilton	1	5	0	Mrs. J. L. Mathewson	0	10	0
Jas. Hardman	1	5	0	" John Mathewson	0	5	0
Benjamin Dawson	1	5	0	" J. A. Mathewson	0	5	0
Wm. Riley	1	5	0	" Bennett	0	5	0
G. E. Jaques	1	5	0	" Jenking	0	5	0
John Gardner	0	10	0	" Outhet	0	5	0
C. Beatty	0	5	0	" Hale	0	5	0

ST. JAMES STREET METHODIST CHURCH. 85

Contributions to the Wesleyan Missionary Society from St. James St. Church, Montreal.

Year.	Amount.		
1819	£62	0	0
1820	50	0	0
1821	36	0	0
1822	50	0	0
*1823			
*1824			
1825	91	16	0
1826	120	0	0
1827	3	2	9
1828	175	0	11
1829	109	3	6
1830	130	18	9
1831	188	8	6
1832	157	19	8
1833	160	4	0
1834	21	14	10
1835	156	6	10
1836	185	7	7
1837	198	2	11
1838	224	17	3
1839	300	11	6
1840	235	0	6
1841	255	4	8
*1842			
*1843			
1844	339	6	5
1845	313	11	7
1846	355	13	1
1847	368	19	2
1848	362	13	10
1849	250	0	0
1850	229	6	11
1851	225	0	0
1852	263	7	2
1853	249	13	1
1854	232	0	5
1855			

* No detailed returns included in Eastern Canada.

Year.	Amount.
1856	$1,122 73
1857	1,110 15
1858	1,110 57
1859	1,094 60
1860	1,049 46
1861	1,041 88
1862	2,893 02
1863	5,280 90
1864	4,483 69
1865	2,500 25
1866	3,652 35
1867	3,803 10
1868	3,758 06
1869	4,049 41
1870	4,022 53
1871	4,350 75
1872	5,183 47
1873	5,604 35
1874	5,275 94
1875	6,160 71
1876	5,084 58
1877	4,800 12
1878	3,847 34
1879	3,115 18
1880	3,259 22
1881	3,604 88
1882	3,692 85
1883	3,767 73
1884	3,190 19
1885	3,253 05
1886	3,179 92
1887	2,985 85

ST. JAMES STREET METHODIST CHURCH. 87

Juvenile Missionary Subscriptions.

Year.	St. James' Schools.	Total Juvenile for City.
1851	$83 26	$236 93
1852	171 67	445 59
1853	132 87	461 77
1854	132 87	461 77
1855	210 76	547 81
1856	242 87	549 27
1857	240 00	550 00
1858	242 87	549 27
1859	203 58	512 38
1860	228 08	530 37
1861	282 73	641 85
1862	304 95	707 25
1863	338 37	811 48
1864	252 80	877 50
1865	320 23	906 02
1866	400 00	1,000 00
1867	500 00	1,296 61
1868	500 80	1,710 82
1869	600 42	1,792 64
1870	649 40	2,001 08
1871	737 39	2,377 36
1872	993 75	2,530 66
1873	1,397 70	3,154 32
1874	2,032 52	3,974 34
1875	1,793 15	3,498 07
1876	1,543 57	3,011 78
1877	1,118 79	2,378 65
1878	817 05	2,319 19
1879	1,075 47	2,812 07
1880	1,317 82	3,126 91
1881	1,461 81	3,324 06
1882	1,257 45	3,479 51
1883	1,421 96	3,304 94
1884	1,416 36	3,436 48
1885	1,765 04	4,154 80
1886	1,743 05	4,657 01
1887	1,112 86	4,373 82
Total	$29,046 27	$72,504 38

Net Debt on the Church Property at the Close of Each Year.

Year.	Amount.	Increase.	Decrease.	Cause.
1867.	$35,014 00	....	....	
1868	33,205 00		$1,809 00	
1869	31,787 00		1,418 00	
1870	29,668 00		2,119 00	
1871	30,612 00	$944 00		Grant to East End Church of $1.36i, otherwise decrease of $2,4.e.
1873	44,160 00	13,546 00	....	Grant to College.
1874	41,687 00		2,473 00	
1875	41,213 00		474 00	
1876	38,299 00	....	2,914 00	
1877	37,726 00	....	573 00	
1878	38,308 00	582 00		
1879	42,303 00	3,995 00	....	Addition to stores adjoining church.
1880	41,235 00	....	1,068 00	
1881	41,510 00	275 00	....	
1882	41,549 00	39 00	....	
1883	40,879 00	....	670 00	
1884	41,549 00	670 00	....	
1885	42,703 00	1,154 00	....	Repairs St. Paul St. property.
1886	41,344 00		1,359 00	

ST. JAMES STREET METHODIST CHURCH. 89

Contributors to the Building Fund of the First St. James Street Church, Built in 1820.

J. Atkinson.
Joseph Allan.
R. Armour.
A. Burberry.
A. Bagg.
W. Brown.
Joseph Chapman.
Chalmers & Granin.
F. Chapman.
S. B. Cobb.
J. Carmell.
W. Cheney.
J. Colt.
H. Dickinson.
James Douglas.
Dougall & McMillan.
Alex. Downie.
J. N. Dwight.
P. Diehl.
Mr. Donegani.
Mr. Dunn.
Jacob Dewitt.
Jabez Dewitt.
Kenneth Dowie.
D. Fisher.
Miss Nancy Fisher.
John Fisher, sen.
D. & J. Fisher.
John Fleming.
J. M. Frothingham.
John Frothingham.
S. Finchley.
J. French.
A. Ferguson.

J. Foulke.
James Foster.
Gibbs & Kollmyer.
A. & H. Gilbert.
F. Gunnerman.
James Greerfield.
H. Gates.
Mrs. Hutchinson.
J. & J. Henshaw.
James Henderson.
Mrs. Hall.
N. Handyside.
Nahum Hall.
Mrs. Jane Hick.
Isaac Jones.
Kent & White.
N. P. Kurcyyn.
Wm. Kelly.
F. Leonard.
Wm. Lyman.
Wm. Lamb.
Wm. Lang.
Wm. Lunn.
R. McGinnis.
G. McDonald.
J. Mitzler.
Mrs McKay.
N. McDonald.
D. McLaughlin.
D. McLean.
John McKenzie.
Adam Miller.
Nahum Mower.
Joseph Masson.

Andrew Noel.
Charles Penner.
J. C. Pierce.
Andrew Porteous.
Dr. Pomroy.
Wm. Reed.
Daniel Robertson.
C. Russell & Co.
Mr. Richardson.
Wm. Smith.
J. R. Spottiswood.
John Sandford.
John Spittal.
W. & J. Spragg.
Miss Seyers.
James Somerville.
James Shuter.
A. Smythe.
John Torrance.
John Try.
Charles Try.
R. Taylor.
J. A. Turner.
Mr. Tait.
A. Thyer.
E. C. Tuttle.
Ware & Gibb.
R. Walker.
Wm. Walker.
Woolwich & Symes.
W. T. Wilson.
J. Woolwich.
A. White.
W. Wilkins.

Contributors to the Building Fund, 1846.

Trustees.

Hon. James Ferrier	£400	0 0
Wm. Lunn	300	0 0
Thomas Kay	125	0 0
John Mathewson	100	0 0
David Torrance	100	0 0
Robert Campbell	100	0 0
John Torrance	50	0 0
Richard Latham	50	0 0
John Hilton	50	0 0
	£1,275	0 0

George Armstrong.
E. Atkinson.
Samuel Ash.
Thomas Wm. Allan.
Bryson & Ferrier.
Edmund Baird.
James Brattin.
Wm. Bennett.
Adolphus Bourne.
J. M. Barlow.
W. Black.
Robert Benn.
Elizabeth Best.
Ann Beattie.
Bryson & Campbell.
Joshua Bell.
Dr. Bernard.
Francis Bethell.
John Barry.
John Burnard.
Wm Berry.
Mrs. Barry.
G. W. Campbell, M.D.
Moses Carter.
George Culver.
W. H Clifford.
J Craig.
Francis Coy.

Wm. Dyer.
Joseph Dyer.
John Dyer.
John Douglas, sen.
John Douglas, jun.
James Douglas.
George Douglas.
R. Everett.
John Eward.
Mrs. Eward.
Wm. Fager.
Wm. Eaton.
Arthur Fisher, M.D.
Joseph Fox.
James Ferrier, jun.
Thomas Francis.
Margaret Francis.
F. Fraser.
James Foster.
Samuel Foley.
Mr. Fenton.
Wm. Gettes.
Robert Graham.
John Gunn.
Eleanor Gaw.
Samuel Galway.
Joseph Gouldthorpe.
George Gabding.

George Harrison.
George Horne.
Henry Horne.
Daniel Hadley.
Francis Hadley.
Joseph Horner.
C. T. Howith.
John Hutchinson.
Henderson Bros.
Miss Mary Hillock.
John Holland.
Richard Holland.
Robert Irwin.
Mrs. Illsley.
John Illsley.
Thomas Jenking.
Wm. King.
J. R. Kirkwood.
Miss King.
R. Kneeshaw.
Miss Kirkwood.
John Lewis.
Miss Lunn.
George Loughlin.
Thomas Little.
Thomas Mathers.
John Miller.
John McComb.

ST. JAMES STREET METHODIST CHURCH. 91

S. & D. Milligan.
R. H. Mathewson.
Samuel Mathewson.
J. A. Mathewson.
Mathewson & Sinclair.
R. W. L. McKay.
Rev. James Osgood.
Wm. Pawson.
James Patton.
Mrs. James Patton.
James Patton, jun.
Samuel Patton.
John Patton.
T. J. Pape.
Wm. Patrick.
Thomas Rattray.
James Robinson.
Richard Rogers.
John Robson.
George Robson.

R. Ruston.
Rev. M Ritchie.
E. Reynolds.
John Ransom.
Rogers & Wright.
Mrs. Rogers.
Wm. Smith.
Mrs. W. Smith.
Thomas Smith.
J. W. Smith.
Wm. Scholes.
Charles Schrimpton.
James Struthers.
John Sinclair.
Mrs. John Sinclair.
Wm. Shaw.
Edna Stevenson.
John Sproston.
Joseph Simmers.
John Stephen.

J. Skelton.
Robert Smith.
Mrs. Sarah Stephens.
R. Smith, of Bacup, Eng.
Mrs. David Torrance.
Mrs. John Torrance.
John A. Torrance.
David Tees.
Wm. Tabb.
John Tees.
Robert Tweedie.
Wm. Taylor.
George Wandby.
Jane Watson.
James Weeks.
George Watson.
John W. Watson.
Mrs. Wright.
Richard Yates.

Abstract Statement of Receipts of the Trustees from the Opening of Church, 1846, until May 14th, 1886.

Collections at opening of church	$436 57
Sale of old church	17,395 25
Plate collections	33,607 87
Pew rents	105,166 28
Rents of stores and assessments	71,884 02
Subscriptions at opening of church	32,058 28
Special Relief Fund, 1855-61	51,374 88
Ladies in 1856, for debt	274 12
Ladies in 1860, for organ	333 31
Loans and mortgages	265,395 80
Rent of parsonage—1873, '74, '75 ; received from Quarterly Board	900 00
Insurance Company, damage from fire	5,328 66
Interest and dividends	2,257 38
	$586,412 42

ST. JAMES STREET METHODIST CHURCH.   93.

Abstract Statement of Expenditure of the Trustees. from the Opening of Church in 1846, to May 14th, 1886.

Cost of St. James Street Church, in full..	$56,147	68
Expenses of heating, lighting, sexton, music; cost of organs, except the first; repairs to same; extension and repairs of adjoining stores	102,577	74
Interest	88,773	30
Taxes on stores adjoining church	14,960	39
Loans and mortgages paid off	152,726	78
Cost of East End Church, net..$23,401 39		
Cost of Ottawa Street Church . 27,703 90		
Donations to West End Church 2,400 00		
Church extension movement .. 6,300 00		
Grant to Wesleyan Theological College 10,000 00		
Interest on said grant 8,811 31		
	78,616	60
Cost of St. Paul Street property, net	7,277	24
Cost of parsonage, $5,500; improvements, $885.07 .... 6,385 07		
Interest on mortgage on parsonage, improvements, etc. 3,045 00		
	9,430	07
Summer pulpit supply	1,033	40
Bonuses or grants to ministers	3,156	35
Cost of St. Catherine Street property	70,087	95
	$584,787	50
Balance of cash on hand, May 14, 1886	1,624	92
	$586,412	42

Chronology of Montreal Methodism.

1802 First class formed by Rev. Joseph Sawyer, of N. Y. Conference.
1803 First Methodist Minister stationed, Rev. S. Merwin.
1808 First church built.
1815 First Wesleyan Methodist Minister from England, Rev. J. Strong.
1819 First Missionary Auxiliary in Canada formed.
1820 Withdrawal of American Methodist Missionaries.
1821 New Church opened corner St. James and St. François Xavier Streets.
1827 Chapel in Gain Street, Quebec suburbs; class having been organized by John Mathewson in 1826.
1834 January 24, Wellington Church, near McGill Street, opened.
1837 Gain Street congregation moved to St. Mary Street Chapel, which was fitted up by Hon. James Ferrier.
1844 East End Church opened.
1845 St. James Street Church opened.
1847 Wellington Street Church burnt; Ottawa Street opened January 20.
1854 Union of Lower Canada District of British Conference with the Wesleyan Methodist Conference of Canada.
1855 New Connexion Church opened June 28.
1856 Salem, New Connexion in Panet Street opened.
1857 Ebenezer, New Connexion opened in Dupre Lane.
1865 Dominion Square, Sherbrooke Street, and Point St. Charles Churches opened.
1865 St. Lambert Church built.
1867 Temporary building for West End.
1868 Lachine Church built in connection with West End Church.
1869 West End opened.
1870 Cote St. Paul Church, formerly Union, purchased by Methodists.
1873 Wesleyan Theological College founded.
1874 Union of Wesleyan Methodist Conference, New Connexion, and Wesleyan Methodist Church, Eastern British America.
1875 Douglas Church opened.
1878 First French Church opened.
1884 Union of Methodist Church of Canada, Methodist Episcopal Church Primitive Methodist Church, and the Bible Christian Church.
1887 Corner-stone of New Church, St. Catherine Street, laid June 11th.
1888 May 6, Opening Services Mountain St. Church (late Ottawa St.)

ST. JAMES STREET METHODIST CHURCH. 95

Baptisms, Marriages and Deaths.

Year.	Baptisms.	Marriages.	Deaths.
1846	28	9	14
1847	17	4	20
1848	44	21	25
1849	41	32	35
1850	35	31	19
1851	39	25	10
1852	64	35	14
1853	40	41	19
1854	38	28	22
1855	51	29	24
1856	36	28	24
1857	37	9	19
1858	60	13	26
1859	61	15	24
1860	77	23	32
1861	48	21	21
1862	63	19	24
1863	45	25	32
1864	48	13	22
1865	45	21	20
1866	42	27	20
1867	47	25	14
1868	30	31	13
1869	42	27	8
1870	35	13	20
1871	33	21	25
1872	40	27	32
1873	36	21	23
1874	27	21	28
1875	46	30	32
1876	49	26	38
1877	51	20	25
1878	41	16	34
1879	34	19	11
1880	46	21	26
1881	45	15	25
1882	48	22	22
1883	31	31	15
1884	30	20	22
1885	30	14	16
1886	42	25	18
1887	34	20	20
	1376	934	932

Methodist Ministers Stationed in Montreal, with Membership Reported.

American.

Year.	Minister.	Membership.
1802	Joseph Sawyer	7
1803	S. Merwin	7
1804	Martin Ruter	12
1805	" "	20
1806	S. Coates	20
1807	Nathan Bangs	20
1808	T. Maddin	30
1809	J. Scull	28
1810	"	28
1811	J. Mitchell	35
1812	T. Burch	36
1813	"	36

American.   British.

1814	T. Burch	R. Williams	36
1815	"	J. B. Strong	37
1816	W. Brown	"	56
1817	W. Barlow	J. DePutron	67
1818	E Bowen	R. Pope	80
1819	A. Sieger	R. L. Lusher	95
1820	T. Dixon	J. Hick	122

British.

1821	R. L. Lusher	J. Knowlan	119
1822	" "	" "	161
1823	" "	" "	120
1824	H. Pope		151
1825	"		121
1826	R. Alder		121
1827	J. Stinson		133
1828	J. Hick		150
1829	"		155
1830	"		156
1831	Wm. Squire		172

ST. JAMES STREET METHODIST CHURCH. 97

Year.	Minister.	Membership.
1832	Wm. Squire	187
1833	W. Croscombe	350
1834	Wm. Barry	395
1835	W. Lord / M. Richey, D.D.	405
1836	W. M. Harvard / J. B. Selley, M.D	560
1837	R. L. Lusher / E. Botterell	585
1838	R. L. Lusher / R. Hutchinson	510
1839	R. L. Lusher / J. P. Hetherington	420
1840	R. L. Lusher / W. Squire / J. P. Hetherington	384
1841	R. L. Lusher / Wm Squire / John Borland	412
1842	Wm. Squire / John Borland / R. Cooney	566
1843 1844	M. Lang / J. B. Brownall / R. Cooney	720
1845	Matthew Richey, D.D. / C. Churchill / G. H. Davis	770
1846	Matthew Richey, D.D. / C. Churchill / G. H. Davis	803
1847	M. Richey, D.D. / C. Churchill	883
1848	John Jenkins, D.D., LL.D / C. De Wolfe / Lachlin Taylor, D.D	890
1849	John Jenkins, D.D., LL.D / C. De Wolfe	890
1850	" "	880
1851	John Jenkins, D.D., LL.D / Wm. Squire / G. N. A. F. T. Dickson	

7

Year.	Minister.	Membership.
1852	{ John Jenkins, D.D., LL.D Wm. Squire G. N. A. F. T. Dickson George Douglas, D.D., LL.D. }	880
1853	{ John Jenkins, D D., LL.D. Wm. Scott George Douglas, D.D., LL.D. J. H. Bishop }	880

CIRCUITS DIVIDED.

Canadian Ministers.

1854	Wellington Jeffers, D.D	250
1855	" "	250
1856	" "	313
1857	John Gemley	353
1858	" "	376
1859	{ John Gemley Ebenezer Robson }	366
1860	Isaac B. Howard	366
1861	Ephraim B. Harper, D.D.	386
1862	" "	388
1863	" "	585
1864	{ James Elliott, D.D Charles Lavell }	585
1865	{ James Elliott, D.D. William Briggs, D.D }	431

Dominion Square Church, separate Circuit.

1866	James Elliott, D.D	452
1867	{ George Douglas, D.D., LL.D. J. B. Clarkson, M.A. }	485
1868	George Douglas, D.D., LL.D.	298
1869	" "	301
1870	John Potts, D.D	399
1871	"	429
1872	"	448
1873	Alexander Sutherland, D.D	516
1874	{ Alex. Sutherland, D.D. Benj. Longley, B.A. }	487

ST. JAMES STREET METHODIST CHURCH.

Year.	Minister.	Membership.
1875	Leonard Gaetz / Benj. Longley, B.A.	473
1876	Leonard Gaetz	499
1877	" "	533
1878	Hugh Johnston, M.A., B.D.	473
1879	" "	367
1880	" "	402
1881	Delmer E. Mallory	402
1882	John Potts, D.D.	358
1883	" "	400
1884	" "	
1885	John Philp, M.A.	478
1886	" "	518
1887	" "	570
1888	James Henderson	

Total Amounts of Money Raised from Opening of Church, 1846, to May, 1887.

Salaries, 1851-87	$77,925 00
Missionary contribution	124,803 18
Superannuated ministers	15,901 69
Educational Fund, 1855-68	940 86
" " 1873-87	2,566 33
Children's Fund	5,086 16
Church Relief Fund, 1856-74	1,054 73
College Sustentation, 1869-74	738 71
Removal expenses	1,000 00
Sunday-schools, estimated	15,217 35
General Conference Fund	424 73
Ladies' Aid	9,000 00
Poor Fund	13,397 84
Pew rents, 1846-86	107,514 13
Plate collections, 1846-86	34,830 07
Subscription at opening, 1846	32,058 28
Relief Fund, 1855-61	51,374 88
	$493,933 44

ST. JAMES STREET METHODIST CHURCH. 101

Members and Adherents.

Envelope No.	Pew No.	Name.	Residence.
171	..	Adams, A............	343 Visitation St.
24	..	Agnew, Miss Maggie ..	
288	..	Alarde, C. J.........	43 Aylmer St.
..	..	Allen, Marion	20 City Councillors' St.
266	..	Allen, Miss M. E.	"
..	..	Allo, G. H.	15½ St. Margaret St.
46	8	Alston, J. F	15 Lincoln Avenue.
..	..	Alston, Mrs. J. E.	"
..	..	Andrews, Amelia	
207	123 G.	Anderson, W.	110 St. Alexander St.
..	..	Anderson, Mrs........	"
..	..	Anderson, Miss Effie ..	"
..	..	Anderson, —	
11	73	Archibald, Mrs.	260 St. Charles Borrommée St.
..	73	Archibald, Miss Nellie.	" "
..	73	Archibald, Miss Laura .	" "
..	..	Archibald, Jas	
..	..	Archibald, W.	
174	..	Armitage, D. T.	Mile End.
577	22	Armitage, E. H.	18 Brunswick St.
..	..	Armitage, Miss	
261	68	Armstrong, George....	112 St. Luke St.
2	68	Armstrong, Mrs. Geo..	"
278	68	Armstrong, William ..	30 Victoria Square.
279	68	Armstrong, Mrs. W..	"
220	68	Armstrong, Frank ...	"
..	..	Armstrong, Mrs. J	17 David's Lane.
..	..	Armstrong, Miss	
511	..	Armstrong, John	6 Cathedral St.
..	49	Atkinson, T	104 St. Hypolite St.
..	..	Atkinson, Mr.	
..	..	Babcock, Mrs.	1821 Ontario St.
..	..	Babcock, Miss	"
448	43	Babcock, C. S	"
500	43	Babcock, Stewart	"
..	..	Bactman, Miss Eliza ..	175 St. Urbain St.
79	14	Ball, Miss Alice	20 City Councillors' St.
592	..	Barber, A. C.	73 Bleury St.
..	..	Barber, Mr.	96 Fortier St.
..	..	Barr, Robert..........	Drill Hall, Craig St.
..	100	Bastian, Thomas......	14 City Councillors' St.
..	..	Bastian, Miss Clara ..	
432	..	Bateman, Miss E.....	175 St. Urbain St.

Envelope No.	Pew No.	Name.	Residence.
	35	Baxter, Miss E........	19 Brunswick St.
14		Baxter, Miss Eliza	37 City Councillors' St.
		Beek, Jane	514 St. Urbain St.
20	14	Bell, Miss H..........	59 Latour St.
		Bell, John............	158 St. Urbain St.
	14	Bell, John............	59 Latour St.
		Bell, Mrs.	6 Stanley St.
43	14	Bell, Miss Jane	59 Latour St.
		Best, George..........	150 St. Urbain St.
161		Best, Joseph..........	150 St. George St.
263		Biggs, Joseph	Methodist College.
		Birch, Isabella	106 Hypolite St.
532		Blair, Miss Maggie....	
		Bogan, John	33 Park Avenue.
342		Bogan, Mrs. G. M. P..	"
	69	Bonner, John	Dorchester St.
		Bonner, Mrs..........	"
		Boon, Mrs............	214 St. George St.
		Boon, Miss Gertie	"
		Boon, J. W...........	"
		Boon, G. S............	"
6	46	Borland, Rev. John....	298 St. Charles Borrommée St.
371		Borland, Miss	" "
	89	Borland, D. B	
310		Brazier, George	40 Kent St.
495		Brook, Gilbert........	198 Aqueduct St.
	169 G.	Brown, Mrs...........	4 Mount St. Charles Place.
54	38	Brown, W. Godbee....	7 Platt St.
348	38	Brown, Mrs. W. G....	"
		Brown, Robert........	4 Mount St. Charles Place.
120		Brown, Robert........	" "
153		Bryans, John	151 St. Urbain St.
61	26	Bryant, Isaac	21 Latour St.
39		Bulam, Miss Sarah....	155 Union Ave.
		Bunting, Mrs. (Widow)	
221		Burch, Miss Isabella ..	106 Hypolite St.
		Burden, Mrs..........	15 Berthelot St.
		Burden, Hattie........	9 Josephine Lane.
		Burden, Fred.	"
		Burden, Mrs..........	"
16	7	Burdon, Thomas W. ..	50 Park Ave.
62		Burdon. Mrs. T. W. ..	"
	81	Byrd, Mrs............	
	98	Byrd, John	
178		Cameron, Duncan	807 Dorchester St.
303	22	Cameron, Miss Maggie.	42 Union Ave.
526	31	Campbell,Mrs.Dr.G.W.	707 Sherbrooke St.
353	31	Campbell, Miss A. L...	"
		Campbell, Miss H.....	

ST. JAMES STREET METHODIST CHURCH. 103

Envelope No.	Pew No.	Name.	Residence.
3	73	Campbell, Miss Jane	260 St. Charles Borrommée St.
..	48	Canniff, R. P.	Bleury St.
187	..	Carey, Miss H	103 Bleury St.
439	..	Carey, Miss Annie	"
..	56	Carlisle, John	1666 Notre Dame St.
..	..	Carlisle, Miss	" "
..	..	Carter, Miss Mary	Lad. Ben. Inst., Berthelot St.
..	..	Clarke, Mrs. Annie	113 St. Urbain St.
12	..	Clendinning, Miss	169 St. Antoine St.
77	34	Clendinning, Wm.	Palace St.
497	..	Clift, W. E.	400 St. Lawrence St.
572	25	Clogg, J. R.	41 St. Elizabeth St.
591	63	Cockburn, Mrs	113 Nazareth St.
186	65	Cockburn, Miss Kate	"
41	65	Cockburn, Miss Nellie	"
42	65	Cockburn, Miss Eliza	"
..	..	Cohen, Mr	
..	..	Collett, Mrs	191 St. Charles Borrommée St.
..	..	Cook, Miss	60 Union Ave.
..	..	Cook, Miss	"
119	98	Corristine, Mrs. E.	Rear 208 St. Ch. Borrommée St.
142	74	Cowan, John	13 Tupper St.
399	..	Cowan, Mrs. John	"
177	133	Cowie, W	10 Roy Lane.
..	..	Coyle, E	690½ Dorchester St.
..	..	Coyle, Miss Billa	
..	..	Crawford, Miss Annie	159 University Street.
251	..	Crawford, Miss Annie	"
257	..	Crawford, M	35 Hermine St.
..	..	Crothers, Miss Jennie	2307 St. Catherine St.
..	..	Crothers, Miss Kate	72 Victoria St.
	11	Dangerfield, Wm	Dorchester St.
..	11	Dangerfield, Mrs	"
578	..	Dashney, Miss	164 St. Antoine St.
..	..	Date, Mrs	28 Mance St.
..	..	Davidson, W. H	68 Latour St.
212	..	Davidson, Mrs. M.	St. Andrew's Home.
..	35	Davidson, Mrs	564 Lagauchetiere St.
..	..	Davidson, Mrs	
222	..	Davidson, Miss Elin	22 St. Monique St.
..	110 G.	Davidson, J	
193	..	Davis, Wm. M	24 Desrivieres St.
234	..	Davis, Mrs. J.	174 Fulford St.
..	9	Dawson, Mrs.	499 Dorchester St.
..	..	Dawson, Miss Carrie	"
..	..	Dawson, Miss A.	"
..	..	Dawson, Miss Alicia	"
..	..	Dawson, Wallace	"
..	..	Dawson, R.	88 Park Ave.

Envelope No.	Pew No.	Name.	Residence.
		Dawson, Mrs.	88 Park Ave.
		Dawson, Mary	"
173	60	Dawson, A. O.	"
		Dawson, Miss Clara	12 Plateau St.
		Dawson, Miss Clara	
255		Day, Miss Lucy	214 Drummond St.
	8	Dean, W.	
		Dean, Mrs. J.	618 Lagauchetiere St.
373		Dice, Miss E	172 St. Antoine St.
	122 G.	Dickson, C.	
	159 G.	Dier, Miss	
		Dixon, George	
324	96	Donaghy, John	St. Catherine St.
		Donaghy, Mrs.	
476		Doran, Mrs.	21 St. Edward St.
	23	Douglas, Rev. G., D.D., LL.D.	228 University St.
413		Douglas, Mrs.	"
		Douglas, Miss	"
		Douglas, Miss Mina	"
		Douglas, Miss Alice	"
183		Dudgeon, John	St. Antoine St.
		Dudgeon, John	454 Guy St.
		Dunbar, Mrs.	28 Windsor St.
		Dunn, J. H.	
313		Duponte, R.	21½ St. Alexander St.
	2	Eaves, Wm.	
126		Edmonson, J	
126		Edmundson, David	571 Lagauchetiere St.
		Elliott, Miss Sophia	3 Charlotte St., Longueuil.
		Elliott, Miss Maggie	" "
		Emery, Phœbe	344 Mountain St.
		Ennis, Maria	328½ St. Lawrence St.
		Evans, Mrs. Janet	House of Ind., Long Point.
50	92	Evans, Alfred	256 St. Charles Borrommée St.
63	92	Evans, Robert	" "
64	92	Evans, Alfred D.	" "
398	32	Fairman, Frederick	116 Mackay St.
398	32	Fairman, Mrs. F.	"
1	1	Ferrier, Hon. James	100 St. Alexander St.
13	4	Ferrier, A. Grant	St. Catherine St.
478	4	Ferrier, Mrs George	"
		Ferrier, Miss Helen	"
		Ferrier, Miss Emily	"
		Ferrier, Mrs. James	144 Metcalfe St.
		Ferrier, Miss Florence	"
		Ferrier, Miss Alice	"
	6	Ferrier, James, jun.	"

ST. JAMES STREET METHODIST CHURCH. 105

Envelope No.	Pew No.	Name	Residence
162	..	Fisher, A. J..........	36 St. Elizabeth St.
..	..	Fisher, Mrs...........	"
17	62	Forbes, George........	2078 St. Catherine St.
..	..	Forbes, Mrs. Geo......	
..	..	Fortier, Mrs..........	35½ St. George St.
..	..	Forward, Eliza........	344 Mountain St.
37	158 G.	Foster, Mrs...........	35½ St. George St.
493	..	Foster, A.............	1877 Notre Dame St.
18	88	Fox, Miss Mary	16 St. Margaret St.
229	..	Fradd, Wm. B........	797 St. James St.
..	99	Franklin, Mrs	
245	13	Frost, D. T..........	20 City Councillors' St.
240	13	Frost, Mrs. D. T......	"
..	..	Frost, David	"
..	..	Frost, Miss Minnie....	"
..	..	Frost, Miss Annie	"
..	..	Frost, Miss Carrie	"
..	..	Frost, Miss L.........	"
..	..	Frost, Carlos.........	"
..	..	Galt, Sir Alex. T., K.C.M.G.	290 Mountain St.
..	30	Galt, Lady	"
403	65	Gatehouse, Mrs.......	22 St. Monique St.
..	..	Gatehouse, Miss	
..	..	Gatehouse, Miss	
..	..	Gatehouse, Miss	
..	..	Gates, Mrs. (Widow)..	
574	..	Gates, Mrs. Margaret.	122 St. Antoine St.
..	..	Gault, Miss	88 Fortier St.
205	..	Gawne, Joseph........	
..	..	Geraghty, W.	
125	..	Gillard, Mrs. Jane	159 St. Urbain St.
..	..	Godfrey, Mrs.	49 Juror St.
203	80	Goodier, H.	21 St. Edward St.
..	..	Goodier, Mrs.	"
..	..	Goodier, Miss	"
204	..	Goodier, Miss M	"
..	..	Gordon, Mr...........	
..	26	Gordon, D. V.........	
36	..	Gorley, Mrs...........	33½ St. George St.
..	45	Gowans, C	
..	..	Gowling, Philip	177 Hypolite St.
252	..	Gowling. Mary	214 Mountain St.
..	..	Gowne, Joseph........	119 Mountain St.
..	61	Graham, R.	173 St. Denis St
67	61	Graham, W.....	"
8	61	Graham, Mrs. R	"
350	61	Graham, Miss L	"
375	61	Graham, Miss Ida	"
..	..	Graham, Miss	Pratt St.

106 CHRONICLES OF THE

Envelope No.	Pew No.	Name.	Residence.
..	..	Graham, Miss Ida	St. Catherine St.
..	..	Graham, Mrs.	104 St. Hypolite St.
520	96	Green, John	169 James St.
..	..	Greendale, H.	
146	..	Grev, Miss Mamie	65 Shuter St.
..	39	Griffin, R. T.	300 St. Charles Borrommée St.
241	39	Griffin, James	83 St. Urbain St.
349	39	Griffin, Miss Lillie	"
..	..	Haggart, Miss Jane ..	112 St. Luke St.
213	170 G.	Hamilton, R.	144 St. James St.
..	..	Hammond, Mrs.	
557	..	Hammond, David	339 St. Antoine St.
..	99	Hammond, R.	St. Urbain St.
..	..	Hannay, Mrs.	48 St. Alexander St.
10	..	Hannay, Miss J	"
..	59	Hannay, Miss	
..	.	Hastie, Mrs. Amelia .	259 Aqueduct St.
..	.	Hawkins, Mrs. Mary ..	26 St. Charles Borrommée St.
..	90	Henderson, C.	
..	..	Henderson, Mary....	
..	..	Henry, W.	
..	.	Heros, Mrs Frederica .	
..	..	Hilton, John F.	
..	75	Hilton, Wm.	1827 Ontario St.
4	..	Hilton, E. A.	245 Bleury St.
..	..	Hilton, Edward	1827 Ontario St.
..	..	Hilton, John	8 Tower St.
449	75	Hilton, J. H.	"
.		Hilton, Mrs. J. H.	
..	81	Hische, Miss....	
..	..	Hiscock, Mrs.	
549	..	Hiscock, Miss Mary Jane	43 Tupper St.
393	2	Hodgson, Wm.	9 St. Edward St.
345	2	Hodgson, Miss	"
394	2	Hodgson, Mrs. Wm ..	"
396	2	Hodgson, Miss F.	"
547	40	Hoggard, Mrs	259 St. Urbain St.
..	157 G.	Hoggard, G...	143 St. Constant St.
206	157 G.	Hoggard, Miss Lillie ..	"
7	12	Holland, Richard	St. Catherine St.
.	..	Holland, Mrs. Richard.	"
..	..	Holland, Miss	"
33	.	Holmes, Richard A. ..	41½ Latour St.
407	27	Hood, Thomas D	159 University St.
..	..	Hood, Mrs. T. D	"
314	.	Hooper, Miss Lizzie ..	299 Peel St.
..	40	Hoskins. Miss	8 Beaver Hall.
331	..	Howes, J.............	62 St. James St.
23	..	Hudson, Miss F.	19 St. Monique St.

ST. JAMES STREET METHODIST CHURCH. 107

Envelope No.	Pew No.	Name.	Residence.
..	134 G.	Innes, J.............	
52	89	Jacobson, Mrs	156 St. Dominique St.
152	79	Jaques, G. E.	4 Stanley St.
465	79	Jaques, Mrs. G. E.....	"
466	79	Jaques, Miss Mary....	"
467	79	Jaques, Reginald C....	"
468	79	Jaques, Edward Henry	"
469	.	Jaques, Edna Kate...	"
470	..	Jaques, Winifred Rose.	"
498	..	Johns, Thomas........	30½ City Councillors' St.
189	..	Johnson, Fred. D.....	Y. M. C. A.
236	96	Johnston, C. F.	41 St. Genevieve St.
..	120 G.	Johnston, Henry.....	
..	..	Johnston, Wm........	39 Chaboillez Square.
..	..	Johnston, D. F........	21 Canning St.
..	13	Kearns, F............	
..	13	Kearns, W.	
.	58	Kelly, T. D	
99	..	Kennedy, Miss L......	596 Lagauchetiere St.
563	..	Kermode, John	204 St. Lawrence St.
..	..	Kerr, Margaret	153 University St.
21	..	Kerr, Miss	"
185	133 G.	Kimber, G. S.........	49 Anderson St.
..	..	Kimber. Mrs. Geo. S...	"
180	90	King, Hugh M.	53 Anderson St.
..	..	King, Mrs. H. M......	"
156	93	King, Wm............	66 University St.
.	..	King, Mrs. William ..	"
196	..	King, Charles W......	"
..	..	King, J. C............	"
456	60	Kneen, Thomas	3 Concord St.
34	..	Kyle, Mary	34 St. Alexander St.
..	..	Kyle, Minnie	443 St. Dominique St.
..	..	Kyle, Dolly	"
437	.	Kyle, Mary	394 St. Dominique St.
438	..	Kyle, Bella	"
512	120 G.	Kyle, James..........	
..	..	Kyle, Martha	92 St. Charles Borrommée St.
.	..	Kyle, Mary	
197	..	Lacken, W.	35 Desrivieres St.
49	77	Lamb, George	107 Stanley St.
483	..	Lamb, Mrs. George ..	
..	..	Lambert, Mrs.........	20 Dominion Ave.
..	..	Lambly, J. T.	
..	..	Lambly, Wm. D	Wesleyan Theological College.
184	..	Lamountain, Ivan ...	384 St. James St.
..	..	Lamountain, J. M.	414 Lagauchetiere St.

Envelope No.	Pew No.	Name.	Residence.
320	46	Landon, E. C.	402 St. Lawrence St.
..	..	Lane, Miss	
..	..	Lang, Mrs. Margaret	67 Aylmer St.
..	97	Langby, J.	
..	..	Latham, Miss	116 Mackay St.
..	..	Lauder, Robert	151 St. Urbain St.
..	..	Lauder, Fanny	"
..	..	Lauder, Nellie	"
..	..	Lauder, William	"
447	..	Lawrence, Miss Mary	89 Shuter St.
..	..	Lawrence, Miss	Shuter St.
..	..	Laws, Henry	
..	..	Lawton, Mrs	
503	24	Lawton, F.	Lagauchetiere St.
27	37	Lee, W. L.	20 Windsor St.
28	37	Lee, Mrs. W. L.	"
..	..	LeRossignoe, A. E	
..	..	LeRossignoe, James	
..	..	LeRossignoe Walter	
..	..	LeRossignoe, Mary	
243	70	Longmore, Mrs. M.	45 St. George St.
446	82	Lund, David	32 Hermine St.
248	..	Lundbery, A.	46 Berthelot St.
276	..	Longmore, Miss L.	112 St. Luke St.
596	..	Lister, Nellie	808 Palace St.
..	..	Little, Miss	
..	..	Longmore, Miss M.	
..	..	Lund, Mrs. David	32 Hermine St.
..	..	Lund, Sarah	"
..	..	Lunn, Miss	
..	..	Lutton, Miss	23 Prince Arthur St.
116	3	Mathewson, Jas. Adams	625 Sherbrooke St.
..	..	Mathewson, Mrs. Jas. A.	"
415	60	Marriage, Walter	12 Plateau Ave,
30	80	Marrotte, Mrs. Mary	1161 Mignonne St.
..	..	Marrotte, Mrs.	
..	47	Masterman, W. H	15 Maple Ave.
593	..	Mathews, Mrs	St. James St.
..	..	Mathews, Miss Mary	
..	3	Mathewson, W. B.	8 Platt St.
..	..	Mathewson, S. J	70 Park Ave.
343	3	Mathewson, Miss A. S.	625 Sherbrooke St.
389	3	Mathewson, Miss E.	200 McGill St.
131	..	Matthew, Miss Caroline	175 St Urbain St.
..	..	Maxwell, Miss	6 Desrivieres Ave.
151	10	McBride, Ald. James	356 Mountain St.
163	10	McBride, Mrs. James	"
157	10	McBride, Harry	"
158	10	McBride, Arthur	"

ST. JAMES STREET METHODIST CHURCH. 109

Envelope No.	Pew No.	Name.	Residence.
		McBride, Mrs. Wm....	
155	10	McBride, John T......	Dorchester St.
164	..	McBride, Mrs. J. T. ...	"
40	..	McCann, Mrs.........	160 Dalhousie St.
453	28	McConnell, Dr. J. B...	141 Bleury St.
269	..	McCulloch, Miss Mary.	385 Sherbrooke St.
576	..	McDonald, Miss M....	26 St. Monique St.
	73	McDonald, Miss	
..	..	McFarland, C.........	131 St. Constance St.
..	..	McFarlane, Miss......	100 Alexander St.
		McFarlane, Miss	"
201	..	McFarlane, Christie ..	
..	26	McFarlane, R. F......	
..	..	McLaren, Miss Margt.	Ladies' Benevt. Institution.
..	14	McLaughlin, W.......	[sity.
..	..	McLean, Mrs	St. Catherine St., near Univer-
260	..	McLeod, Miss Maggie .	20 Roy St.
579	..	McMillan, Miss .. .	11 St. Monique St.
25	..	McRiff, Miss Hannah .	85 Mance St.
..	..	McVey, Mrs	6 Desrivieres Ave.
..	124 G.	McVey, Miss	St. Catherine St.
148	28	Miller, Robert	33 Park Ave.
..	..	Miller, Mrs. Robert ..	"
340	28	Miller, Miss Georgina..	"
341	28	Miller, Miss Christina .	"
..	5	Mills, Joseph	116 Champ de Mars St.
..	89	Moore, Miss.........	125 Bleury St.
..	..	Moore, Miss L.......	"
267	..	Moore, Mrs. Louisa ..	660 Craig St.
..	..	Moran, Zena..........	
..	..	Morham, Alice	2600 St. Catherine St.
44	..	Morin, Miss Zina.....	34 University St.
..	..	Morin, Miss Leah	1386 Notre Dame St.
..	40	Morris, W............	44 Mance St.
..	..	Morris, Miss..........	Mance St.
242	..	Morris, Wm.........	85 St. Philip St.
..	64	Morris, Mrs..........	"
..	..	Morris, Miss Clara	"
..	..	Mu, Harriett	120 St. Famille St.
250	..	Munro, John	171 College St.
57	38	Murphy, John	11 St. Edward St.
58	..	Murphy, Fanny	"
86	..	Murphy, Mrs. John ..	"
..	..	Murriage, Mrs. W.....	19 Plateau St.
..	..	Murring, Maggie......	443 St. Dominique St.
26	57	Nash, Frank..........	23½ Balmoral St.
..	..	Nash, Frederick	
..	..	Nash, Catherine	
315	41	Nichol, T., M.D., D.C.L., LL.D.	140 Mansfield St.

Envelope No.	Pew No.	Name.	Residence.
..	..	Nichol, W., M.D	140 Mansfield St.
387	41	Nichol, Mrs	"
..	..	Nichol, Thos. S	"
386	41	Nichol, Miss	"
..	..	Nimmo, Mr.	
..	..	Nimmo, Miss	
		Osborne, Mrs.	67 St. Charles Borrommée St.
		Osborne, Maud	"
		Osborne, Nellie	"
		Owens, T. A	328½ St. Lawrence St.
		O'Hara, R	
81	..	Palmer, W. C.	9 St. Edward St.
554	..	Parker, D	71 Germain St.
274	25	Parker, W. O. N	7 Hanover St.
91		Parks, J. G.	197 St. James St.
..	35	Parks, J. G.	
..	..	Patterson, Hugh	170 Canning St.
140	171 G.	Patterson, H.	"
..	..	Patterson, Sarah	132 Germain St.
..	..	Patterson, Mrs. Jane	20 Margaret St.
582	..	Patton, Mrs. R.	30 Mance St.
..	..	Patton, John	Mance St.
..	..	Patton, Miss	"
.	..	Patton, Miss	"
..	33	Patton, Mrs	2327½ St. Catherine St.
..	..	Patton, Herbert	
..	.	Peacock, W	7 St. Edward St.
..	..	Peacock, Eleanor	"
..	..	Peacock, Jennie	"
..	..	Pennoch, J.	
..	..	Perry, E. T.	17 St. Charles Borrommée St.
..	..	Perry John	573 Craig St.
262	70	Phillips, James	40 Albert St.
528	..	Phillips, Mrs.	"
..	..	Phillips, Mrs.	2081 Notre Dame St.
..	..	Phillips, Mrs. Margaret	"
545	..	Pickard, W.	196 St. Antoine St.
542	..	Pickard, Mrs. W	"
304	..	Pillow, Mrs.	554 Dorchester St.
228	59	Place, S. S.	621 St. James St.
..	..	Place, Sarah	"
194	..	Pollock, Miss Annie	100 University St.
289	..	Pollock, Miss Mary	
..	13	Pratt, A. P.	
590	..	Pratt, Thomas A	64 Beaver Hall Terrace.
..	..	Pratt, Mrs	64 Beaver Hall Hill.
530	..	Prince, E.	28 Latour St.

ST. JAMES STREET METHODIST CHURCH. 111

Envelope No.	Pew No.	Name.	Residence.
373	..	Quail, Mrs	79 Juror St.
273		Ramby, Elizabeth ..	St. Jean Baptiste Village.
377		Ray, Miss Annie	245 Bleury St.
..	111 G.	Reddy, Charles	58 Chenneville St.
587	..	Reid, John	40 Latour St.
306	..	Richardson, Miss C. ..	26 St. James St.
309	..	Richardson, Mrs. S. ..	"
.	.	Richardson, G	36 Victoria Square.
305	121 G.	Richardson, G. J	20 St. James St.
..	..	Richardson, Miss Addie	
510	.	Roberts, Stephen	25 Hermine St.
..	97	Robertson, J	
389	..	Robertson, A.	73 Bleury St.
239	..	Robertson, Mrs.	174 Fulford St.
..	..	Robinson, Jennie	Lagauchetiere St.
247	145 G.	Rodger, J	103 St. Urbain St.
..	..	Rodger, Jane	"
..	70	Rodgers, J H	"
..	88	Rodgers, Miss	
..	..	Ross, W. E.	178 Mountain St.
361	..	Ross, Mrs. Wm. E	"
.	..	Ross, Mrs. John	
543	..	Ross, Douglas	169 St. James' St.
132	..	Rudd, Mrs.	1 St. Elizabeth St.
9	59	Ryan, Thomas	Custom House.
..	.*	Rylbury, Mrs.	160 St. Maurice St.
66	..	Sadler, J.	50 Mance St.
586	..	Sanders, Miss	19 St. Monique St.
580	..	Scott, A.....	446 St. James St.
191	..	Scott, John	544 Dorchester St.
216	92	Scott, Mrs	Lagauchetiere St.
139	94	Seybold, C.	83 Durocher St.
388	..	Seybold, Mrs. C	"
540	..	Shaver, F. N.	6 St Charles Borrommée St.
..	..	Sherman, Mr.	1713 Ontario St.
..	..	Sherman, Mrs	"
292	.	Sherritt, J. R.	
..	..	Shoam, Miss	
..	..	Sim, James	St. Genevieve St.
..	..	Sinclair, J	
480		Simpson, Wm.	413 Mance St.
338		Simpson, Mrs. W.	"
154	7	Smardon, John	50 Park Ave.
..	..	Smardon, Miss	"
297	73	Smardon, W	140 St. Urbain St.
..	..	Smardon, Mrs. W.	St. Catherine St.
188	66	Smith, W. F	55 Anderson St.
..	70	Smith, Miss	

Envelope No.	Pew No.	Name.	Residence.
202	..	Smith, F. G.	23 Argyle Ave.
35	..	Smith, Miss Fanny....	148 Colborne St.
210	..	Smith, James T.	623 St. James St.
..	..	Smith, Florence	104 St. Luke St.
285	..	Smith, Miss Emma ...	90 Cathcart St.
..	..	Smith, Fanny	
..	..	Stacey, John H.	Pt. St. Charles.
434	..	Staton, Miss C.... ..	239 St. Urbain St.
436	..	Staton, Miss B........	"
.	.	Statton, C	St. Lawrence St.
..	..	Statton, B...........	"
517	..	Staveley, J. W.	50 Forfar St.
..	..	Staveley, Maud	"
..	45	Stoddart, R W.	42 Bleury St.
..	42	Strachan, W..	Mackay St.
..	24	Stronge, J............	
..	..	Sugars, Frank	Bleury St.
..	33	Swail, J	
..	71	Switzer, J. H.	
..	..	Switzer, Miss	
..	..	Switzer, Miss Ella	58 Victoria St.
..	..	Sysons, J.	
485	..	Tasker, T	Bank of British North America.
15	63	Thompson, J..........	4 Desrivieres St.
..	..	Thompson, John	"
..	146 G.	Thompson, R..	
133	..	Thompson, Miss Agnes.	
..	..	Timmins, Mrs.........	90 Cathedral St.
71	29	Torrance, John	100 St. Alexander St.
367	29	Torrance, Mrs. John ..	"
..	..	Torrance, John, jun. ..	"
72	29	Torrance, J. Ferrier ..	"
..	49	Tourgis, Alfred	18 Windsor St.
..	..	Tracy, Louis..........	233 St. Charles Borrommée St.
211	..	Tracy, Miss Annie	"
..	..	Tracy, Thomas........	"
..	..	Tracy, Annie	"
..	..	Trenholme, Miss E. H.	
..	..	Ulley, J. J.	34 Bleury St.
..	..	Ulley, Mrs............	"
..	78	Urquhart, J	10 Youville St.
..	..	Urquhart, Mrs..	"
..	..	Urquhart, Miss	"
..	..	Urquhart, Miss	"
..	.	Usherwood, Sarah	61 St. Urbain St.
..	76	Usherwood, J	"
445		Vanneck, Mrs	112 Mackay St.

ST. JAMES STREET METHODIST CHURCH. 113

Envelope No.	Pew No.	Name.	Residence.
65	..	Vibert, John A........	31 Belmont St.
208	..	Vibert, Arthur V. F. .	"
209	..	Vibert, Joseph C......	"
.	..	Vicary, Mrs..........	24 Donegani St.
160	.	Vipond, George	98 University St.
		Vipond, Mrs. George ..	"
84	24	Warcup, Miss	63 Argyle Ave.
179	63	Walker, Robert	613 Dorchester St.
..	..	Ward, J. B.	Rear of 28 Bleury St.
..	..	Ward, Rev. J. B.......	
74	44	Ward, Alfred	Hamilton.
48	..	Wardill, Miss	36 Mance St.
..	67	Warren, J. J	Bonsecours Market.
59	72	Watson, D.	269 St. Urbain St.
...	..	Watson, D., jun	"
.	..	Watson, Miss L.	"
584	..	Waugh, Miss Bella....	
..	..	Westgate, James......	85½ Inspector St.
.	..	Westgate, Mrs........	"
302	21	Wethay, Edgar	9 Victoria St.
400	21	Wethay, Mrs.........	"
372	21	Wethay, Miss Thirza .	"
..	..	Wheeler, Miss	St. Hilaire St.
..	..	Wheeler. Miss........	"
..	98	White, Mrs...........	
.	.	Wight, Mrs.	1666 Notre Dame St
426	109 G.	Wilkes, Edward T	9 Montcalm St.
429	..	Wilkes, Mrs	"
..	..	Wilkins, Hattie	243 Bleury St.
..	..	Wilson, Miss	
..	55	Wilson, Miss	
.	..	Winch, C. H.	
312	..	Woodman, J C.	245 St. Urbain St.
51	..	Woodman, Mrs.	"
.	22	Wright, J............	
167	177 G.	Wright, Jas. A.	29 Dowd St.
168	177 G.	Wright, Mrs..........	"
		Young, Mrs	49 Juror St.

Since the preceding has been in the printers' hands, there have been three events of great importance to our church :—

1st. The death of Hon. James Ferrier.
2nd. The closing services in the old church.
3rd. The decision of the trustees to erect offices on the old site.

It was pathetic that the death of Mr. Ferrier should be coincident with the closing of the church he so greatly loved. He was the prime mover in its erection ; the largest contributor to all its funds during his lifetime ; the Superintendent of the Afternoon Sunday-school during the whole life of the church : the last survivor of the original Board of Trustees ; and he lived long enough that his funeral services with the closing sermons should be the last public services held in the church.

"Undeniably, the most representative layman of the Methodist Church in the Dominion of Canada has fallen. As far back as 1822, then in the prime of his youth, he became associated with the Methodist Church, and was at once appointed a trustee of the old church, the predecessor of that now on St. James Street. The amazing energy as well as the high Christian consecration of the man at once brought him to the front in everything connected with the interests of the Methodist Church. When the capacity of the old building became inadequate, he was the first to lead in the great movement which resulted in the erection of the present St. James Street Church. It was under his individual supervision and tireless energy that the enterprise was brought to a successful completion. This building was no sooner completed than he led the way in the erection of two other churches, in Griffintown and Quebec suburbs respectively. Mr. Ferrier filled almost every office in the Methodist Church open to a layman—as superintendent of the Sunday-school, as leader, as steward, as member of the Central Missionary Committee, and a delegate to the various Conferences of the Connexion. When many hesitated he was pronounced and determined in favor of the union of all the bodies of Methodism in the one Methodist

BLOCK OF OFFICES ON SITE OF OLD CHURCH.

Church of Canada. He was early impressed with the advantages of ministerial education, and was the father and founder of the Wesleyan Theological College affiliated with McGill.

His enthusiasm for the prosperity of our great University, McGill College, knew no bounds. For more than forty years he contributed his means and gave his untiring services to promote her interests. Indeed, whatever tended to promote our weal of the city, the advance of society in moral reform, the spiritual interest of the Church universal, found an advocate and zealous friend in the departed. He was a man of established religious faith, of a rectitude and exalted conscience which scorned compromise with evil; a man of simple piety, of child-like spirit, unchanging in his friendship, ardent in his affections. A great personality has disappeared from the legislatures and from our city, and to the Methodist Church his loss is irreparable. His memory will be cherished by many hearts along the years to come."

Mr. Ferrier died on Wednesday, May 30th, 1888, and was buried on Saturday afternoon, June 2nd, from the St. James Street Methodist Church.

On the day following, the closing exercises of the old church were held. In the morning the pulpit was occupied by Rev. Hugh Johnston, M.A.; in the afternoon the Sunday-school was addressed by Rev. H. Johnston, M.A., Rev. W. I. Shaw, LL.D., and James Adams Mathewson, Esq.; and in the evening, Rev. Dr. Potts preached. All three services were crowded to the full capacity of the church.

The trustees having failed to secure a satisfactory offer for the old property, have decided to erect on the old site a seven-story building of offices. This is a bold move, but one that they feel is done in the best interests of the church. The building will be seven stories on St. James Street and nine on Fortification Lane, and the estimated cost will be $150,000; and we are sanguine enough to hope for sufficient revenue, not only to meet all the interest on cost of construction of the new church, but also to have a surplus as well.

www.ingramcontent.com/pod-product-compliance
Lightning Source LLC
Chambersburg PA
CBHW030404170426
43202CB00010B/1478